Cause & Effect

Intermediate Reading Practice

Second Edition

Patricia Ackert

with **Nicki Giroux de Navarro**

HEINLE & HEINLE PUBLISHERS
A Division of Wadsworth, Inc.
Boston, Massachusetts 02116 U.S.A.

The publication of *Cause & Effect, Second Edition* was directed by the members of the Newbury House Publishing Team at Heinle & Heinle:

Erik Gundersen, **Editorial Director**
John McHugh, **Market Development Director**
Kristin Thalheimer, **Production Editor**

Also participating in the publication of this program were:

Publisher: Stanley J. Galek
Editorial Production Manager: Elizabeth Holthaus
Project Manager: Rachel Youngman, Hockett Editorial Service
Assistant Editor: Karen Hazar
Production Assistant: Maryellen Eschmann
Associate Marketing Manager: Donna Hamilton
Manufacturing Coordinator: Mary Beth Lynch
Photo Coordinator: Martha Leibs-Heckly
Interior Designer: Winston Ford Design
Illustrator: Carol O'Malia
Cover Designer: Kim Wedlake

Photo Credits
Photo credits (page numbers are given in boldface): **1**—The Granger Collection; **55**—Robert Brenner/PhotoEdit; **117**—David Frasier photolibrary (female pilot), Culver Pictures, Inc. (listening to jazz), NY Convention & Visitors Bureau (skyscrapers); **175**—PhotoEdit; **231**—Gary Conner/PhotoEdit

Heinle & Heinle Publishers is a division of Wadsworth, Inc.

Manufactured in the United States of America

Library of Congress Cataloging-in-Publication Data

Ackert, Patricia.
Cause and effect : intermediate reading practice / Patricia Ackert, Nicki S. Giroux de Navarro. — 2nd ed.
p. cm.
Includes index.
ISBN 0-8384-3814-8
1. English language—Textbooks for foreign speakers. 2. Readers.
I. Navarro, Nikki Giroux de. II. Title.
PE 1128.A296 1994
428.6'4—dc20 93-42859
CIP

Contents

To the Student

There are many advantages to learning English. One is that you can read information about thousands of subjects. There is more information printed in English than in any other language. In this book you will read about some of the topics that are found in English language magazines, newspapers, and books. At the same time, you will increase your knowledge of English.

To the Instructor

Cause & Effect, Second Edition, is an intermediate reading skills text designed for students of English as a second or foreign language who know the basic structures of English and who have a vocabulary of roughly 2000 English words. The text groups 25 highly-engaging reading selections into 5 themes of universal interest.

Cause & Effect is one in a series of three reading skills texts. The complete series has been designed to meet the needs of students from the beginning to the high intermediate level and includes the following:

- *Facts & Figures, Second Edition* .... beginning
- *Cause & Effect, Second Edition* .... intermediate
- *Thoughts & Notions* .... high intermediate

In addition to the student text, an instructor's manual with answers to all the exercises is available. The manual also includes a test for each unit.

• **Pedagogical Design.** The central goal of *Cause & Effect* is to help students develop the critical reading skills they will need for academic, personal, and/or career purposes. Toward this end, each unit offers a comprehensive program that begins with pre-reading questions, continues with reading and discussion, and proceeds through a set of carefully sequenced post-reading exercises.

By any standard, the range of exercise types in *Cause & Effect* is rich and varied. This text provides students with practice in comprehension, building vocabulary, making inferences, finding the main idea, determining cause and effect, scanning, summarizing, paraphrasing, and understanding the sequence of events, and learning to work more effectively with two-word verbs, compound words, connecting words, and noun substitutes. Each unit ends with a guided writing exercise that directs students toward an understanding of the critical link between reading and writing.

• **Teaching Methods.** The lessons in this book should be done in order because vocabulary is introduced gradually, repeated several times in the lesson where it first appears, and repeated in later lessons. Also, some of the exercises build to become more difficult; for example, the summary exercises start with selecting the sentence that best summarizes a paragraph and end with the students writing a summary of the whole reading selection. In addition, the directions given for each exercise are more detailed at first; the directions in later lessons are briefer and may refer back to the detailed instructions given in earlier lessons.

It is suggested that the instructor assign the reading text and some of the exercises for each lesson. The pre-reading questions and illustration at the beginning of each lesson are designed to stimulate the students' interest in the topic and to help them recall anything they might already know. The answers to these pre-reading questions are sometimes general knowledge and sometimes found in the illustration or in the reading text. Pre-reading questions are for discussion only. They should be discussed briefly when the reading is assigned. For most of the exercises, the students can write the answers in the book, and the instructor can go over them with the students in class, explaining or elaborating as necessary. At first, probably just the text, the vocabulary exercises, and possibly the comprehension and main idea exercises will be enough for one assignment. By the middle of the book, the students should be able to do a whole lesson, or a little less if written work is assigned.

The guided writing section at the end of each unit gives students extra practice in writing. The teacher may assign some or all of the questions. The teacher should provide guidance on how to do this exercise, for example, as a journal entry or as a more formal composition. The comprehension questions may also be given as written assignments. The students should answer in complete sentences and use their own words as much as possible. If they do the exercises orally in class, they should make notes in the book and then give a complete sentence from the notes rather than reading the answer directly from the text.

Other exercises can also provide writing practice. The first few main idea and summary exercises are multiple choice, but then the students have to write their own sentences. One method of going over these exercises is for several students to put their sentences on the board and the class can then discuss which are best. However, this would probably be too time-consuming for the last unit where students write a summary of the whole text. The cause/effect and statement/reason exercises can be written assignments too.

Students also need a lot of practice in using the context to understand new words. It is suggested that when assigning a new lesson, the instructor save some class time to select sentences that clearly give the meaning of vocabulary items and have students tell what the words mean. The context clue exercises in the first two lessons teach the students how to do this.

Vocabulary items in the text are bolded. The meanings of many of them can be determined from the context. Vocabulary words in the text that are underlined are glossed or illustrated. Most of the vocabulary is useful, general vocabulary that the students should learn. The instructor should stress that the students must learn the vocabulary by the end of the lesson. The first lesson suggests that the students underline (or highlight) words they don't know and then test themselves when they finish the lesson.

We hope that the students will find the exercises useful in expanding their knowledge of the English language and that they will find the information as interesting as we did when we researched the book.

- **Instructor's Manual.** The student text for *Cause & Effect, Second Edition*, is accompanied by a comprehensive instructor's manual. This teacher's companion includes pedagogical notes, an answer key for the student text, and tests for each of the five units presented in *Cause & Effect*.

The unit tests include a new reading selection with comprehension and main idea questions, general questions on the reading selections in the unit, and questions on the exercise material in the book. There are also short quizzes on the first two lessons for instructors who want to test their students during the first week or two of classes.

Acknowledgments

I would like to thank several people for their help in writing this book. Chris Hasegawa, junior high school science teacher and CPR instructor for the American Heart Association, advised me on the science and CPR lessons. Dr. J. D. Garcia, physics professor at the University of Arizona, advised me on the photovoltaic lesson, and Dr. Leland Pederson, geography professor at the University of Arizona, helped me with the lesson on rain forests. Susan Ward from the UN Center in Tucson supplied materials and assistance for the lesson on "Women and Change." All of these people were most helpful in providing information and reviewing the lessons after I wrote them.

—Patricia Ackert

I would like to add my thanks to Dr. William Rathje of the Anthropology Department at the University of Arizona and his colleague Dr. Susan Dobyns for their gracious assistance on "The Garbage Project." They were generous with their time and expertise on the interview lessons, as was Paul Henri Giroux, musician and authority on jazz. Mr. Giroux is retired from Everett Community College in Everett, Washington. Dr. Paul Boswell of Lakeland College in Tokyo, Japan, also helped me research material, as did my husband, Luis A. Navarro. Finally, thanks go to Mr. Briggs Ackert for all of his editorial help. It has been a pleasure working with all of these people.

—Nicki Giroux de Navarro

Unit 1

Explorers

Alexandra David-Neel

Burke and Wills—Across Australia

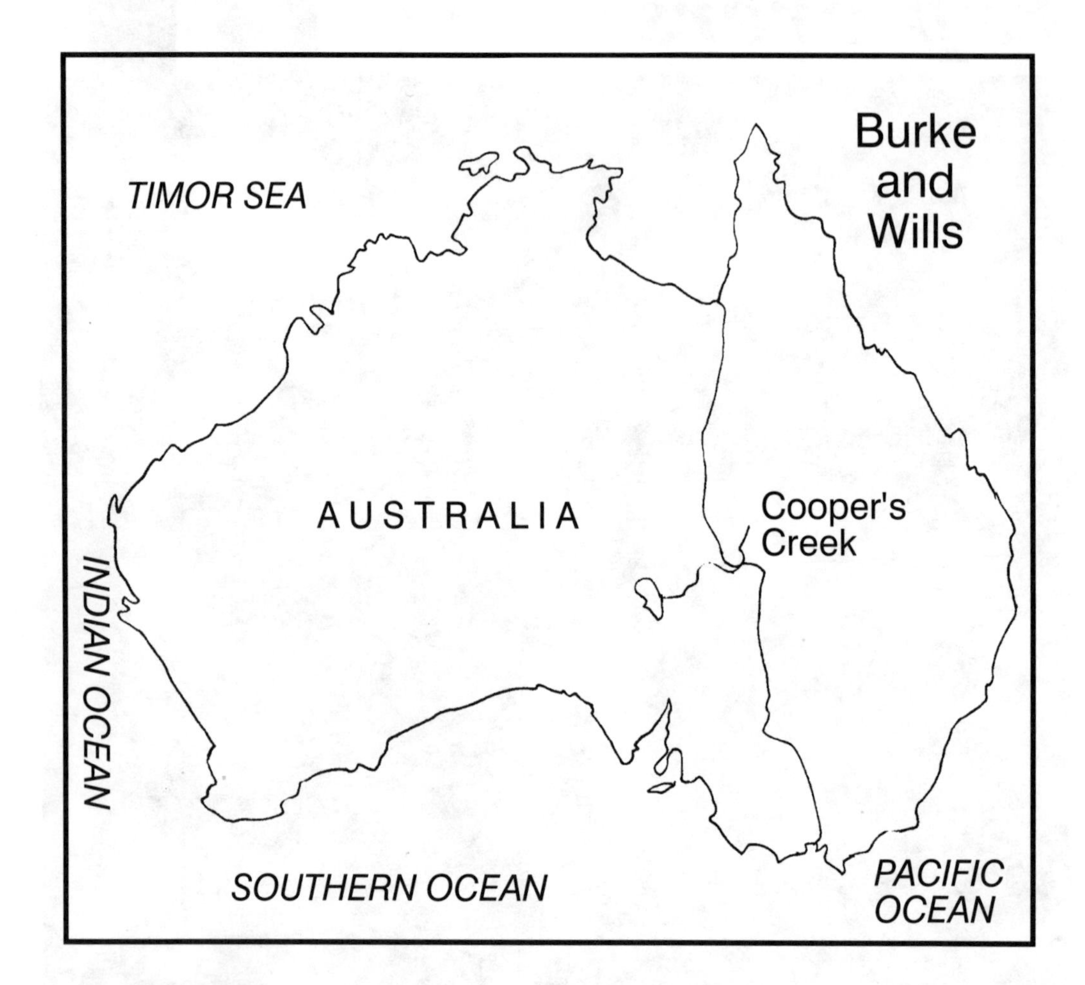

LESSON

Pre-reading Questions

1. **Is August summer or winter in Australia?**
2. **Do camels live in Australia?**
3. **Is Australia larger or smaller than your country?**

1

Burke and Wills—Across Australia

Australia is a **huge** country, and the outback (the Australian word for the **interior** of the country) is desert. In some years, it rains only 8 centimeters in the outback, but in other years, rainstorms **turn** the desert **into** sandy **swamps**.

Until the eighteenth **century**, only **aborigines** lived in Australia. These are the first people who lived in Australia. When Europeans went there to live, they built towns on the coast. However, by the 1850s, people began thinking more about the interior.

In 1860, Robert O'Hara Burke, a police officer from Ireland, was **chosen** to lead an **expedition** across the **continent** from south to north. He took with him William John Wills and eleven other men, camels, horses, and enough **supplies** for a year and a half. They left Melbourne for the Gulf of Carpentaria on August 20, winter in the southern **hemisphere**.

The expedition had problems from the beginning. Burke had no **experience** in the outback. The men fought and would not follow orders. Twice they left some of their supplies so they could move faster and later sent one of the men, William Wright, back for them.

huge: very large
interior: inside, away from the coast
turn into: change into, become
century: 100 years
chosen: past participle of *choose*
supplies: food and other necessary things
hemisphere: half of the earth

Finally, a small group led by Burke moved on **ahead** of the others to a river named Cooper's Creek and set up their **base** camp. They were halfway across the continent, but it was summer now, with very hot weather and sandstorms.

They waited a month for Wright, and then Burke decided that four from his small group, with 3 months' supplies, should travel the 1250 kilometers to the north coast as quickly as possible. They told the others to wait for them at Cooper's Creek.

The **journey** across the desert was very difficult, but at the end of January, they reached the Flinders River near the Gulf of Carpentaria.

They started their return journey, but now it was the rainy season and traveling was slow and even more difficult than on their trip north. They did not have enough food, and the men became hungry and sick. Then one of them died. Some of the camels died or were killed for food.

Finally, on April 21, they arrived back at Cooper's Creek, only to find that no one was there. The rest of the expedition left the day before because they thought Burke must be dead.

The men continued south, but without enough food, both Burke and Wills died. Aborigines helped the last man who was still alive, and a **search party** found him in September 1861. He was half crazy from hunger and loneliness.

search = look for,
party = a group of people

There were many reasons that the expedition did not go as it was planned. It had an inexperienced leader, the men made bad **decisions**, some did not follow orders, and they did not **get along**. But they were the first expedition to cross Australia, and Burke and Wills are still known as **heroes** of **exploration**.

noun for *decide*

be friendly, not fight

A Vocabulary

In this book, difficult words are repeated several times in the exercises. These words are also repeated and reviewed in other lessons. It is not necessary to list new English words with their meanings in your own language. You will learn them just by practicing. In each lesson, when you read the text the first time, underline the words that you don't know. Then you can give yourself a test when you finish the lesson. Look at the words you underlined and see if you understand them. If you don't know them yet, this is the time to memorize them.

In the vocabulary exercises in this book, write the correct word in each blank. Use each word only once. Use capital letters where they are necessary.

exploration	decision	hemisphere	experience
continents	ahead	expedition	century
aborigines	gets along	base	heroes

1. Please decide what you want to do. You must make a ________________.
2. In baseball, a player hits the ball and runs to first ________________.
3. The first Australians are called ________________.
4. Do you have any ________________ as a secretary, or is this your first job?
5. Kumiko ________________ well with everyone. She is always nice and never fights with people.
6. The years 1900–1999 are the twentieth ________________.
7. Tom saw some children ________________ of him in the street while he was driving home, so he slowed down.
8. Asia is in the northern ________________.
9. Africa, Antarctica, Asia, Australia, Europe, North America, and South America are the seven ________________.
10. People who win in the Olympic Games are ________________ in their countries.

B Vocabulary

Do this exercise like Exercise A.

chosen	expedition	experience	exploration
huge	interior	journey	party
searching	supplies	swamps	turned into

1. Burke and Wills led an ________________ into the interior of Australia.
2. Christopher Columbus was ________________ for a new way to go to India.
3. Canada is a ________________ country, one of the biggest in the world.
4. Birds like to live in ________________ because there is a lot of water and food.
5. We use one kind of paint for the ________________ of a house and another kind for the exterior.
6. It is a long ________________ from Melbourne to London.
7. A search ________________ was sent to find the Burke and Wills expedition.
8. Most of the earth has been explored. Now we are in the age of space ________________, searching for more information about the stars, the moon, and other planets besides Earth.
9. The secretary ordered paper, pens, and other ________________ for the office.
10. Carlos started to study hard and ________________ a good student.

C True/False

Write **T** if the sentence is true. Write **F** if it is false. If a question is false, change it to make it true, or explain why it is false.

An asterisk (*) before a question means it is either an **inference** or an **opinion** question. You cannot find a sentence in the text with the answer. You have to use the information in the text and things you already know and then decide on the answer.

______ 1. The first Europeans in Australia built villages in the outback because there were too many aborigines on the coast.

_______ 2. The Burke and Wills expedition crossed Australia from south to north.

_______ *3. December is a summer month in Australia.

_______ 4. Much of the interior of Australia is swampy all year long.

_______ 5. Eleven men crossed Australia with Burke and Wills.

_______ *6. Burke and Wills did not have enough food for their journey back to Cooper's Creek because the rain slowed them down.

_______ *7. The aborigines could help the last man still alive because they understood how to live in the desert.

_______ 8. Burke was a good leader for this expedition.

D Comprehension Questions

Answer these questions in complete sentences. An asterisk (*) means it is either an **inference** or an **opinion** question. **You cannot find the exact answer in the text.**

1. Where did the first Europeans live when they went to Australia?

*2. Why were camels good animals for this expedition?

3. Why did the men leave some of their supplies behind them?

4. Why was it difficult to travel in the interior of Australia?

5. What happened to some of the camels?

6. Name two reasons why this expedition had so many problems.

*7. Do you think Burke and Wills should be called heroes of exploration? Why?

E Main Idea

What is the main idea of paragraph 4 (lines 20–25)?

1. Robert Burke led this expedition.
2. The expedition had many problems.
3. Burke had no experience in the outback.

F Two-Word Verbs

English has many two-word verbs. Each of the two words is easy, but when they are put together, they mean something different. There is often no way to guess what they mean. You have to learn each one. Learn these two-word verbs and then fill in the blanks with the right words. Use the correct verb form.

turn into —change into, become
get along (with)—not fight, be friendly
break down —to stop going or working (often about a car)
call on —when someone, usually a teacher, asks someone to speak
put away —put something in the place where it belongs

1. Our washing machine ________________ yesterday and I couldn't finish washing my clothes.
2. Tommy and his little brother don't ________________ very well. They fight about something almost every day.
3. Ali knew the answer when the teacher ________________ him.
4. It was rainy this morning, but now it has ________________ a beautiful day.
5. Mary doesn't usually ________________ her clothes. She just leaves them on a chair or the bed.

G Articles (a, an, the)

There are so many rules about articles that it is easier just to get used to them by practicing than to learn all the rules. However, you will learn a few of the rules later in this book. Here are some sentences or parts of sentences from the text. Put an article in the blank if it is necessary.

1. In other years, rainstorms turn ______ desert into sandy swamps.
2. Until ______ eighteenth century, only aborigines lived in ______ Australia.
3. In 1860, ______ Robert O'Hara Burke, ______ police officer from Ireland, was chosen to lead ______ expedition across ______ continent from south to north.

4. He took with him William John Wills, _____ eleven other men, _____ camels, _____ horses, and enough supplies for _____ year and _____ half.
5. _____ expedition had _____ problems from _____ beginning.
6. _____ men fought and would not follow _____ orders.

H Guided Writing

Write one of these two short compositions.

1. You are the last person still alive from the Burke and Wills expedition. It is September 1861, and the search party has just found you. Tell them what happened to you.

2. You are the leader of another expedition across Australia. Explain what you will do differently.

Alexandra David-Neel— A French Woman in Tibet

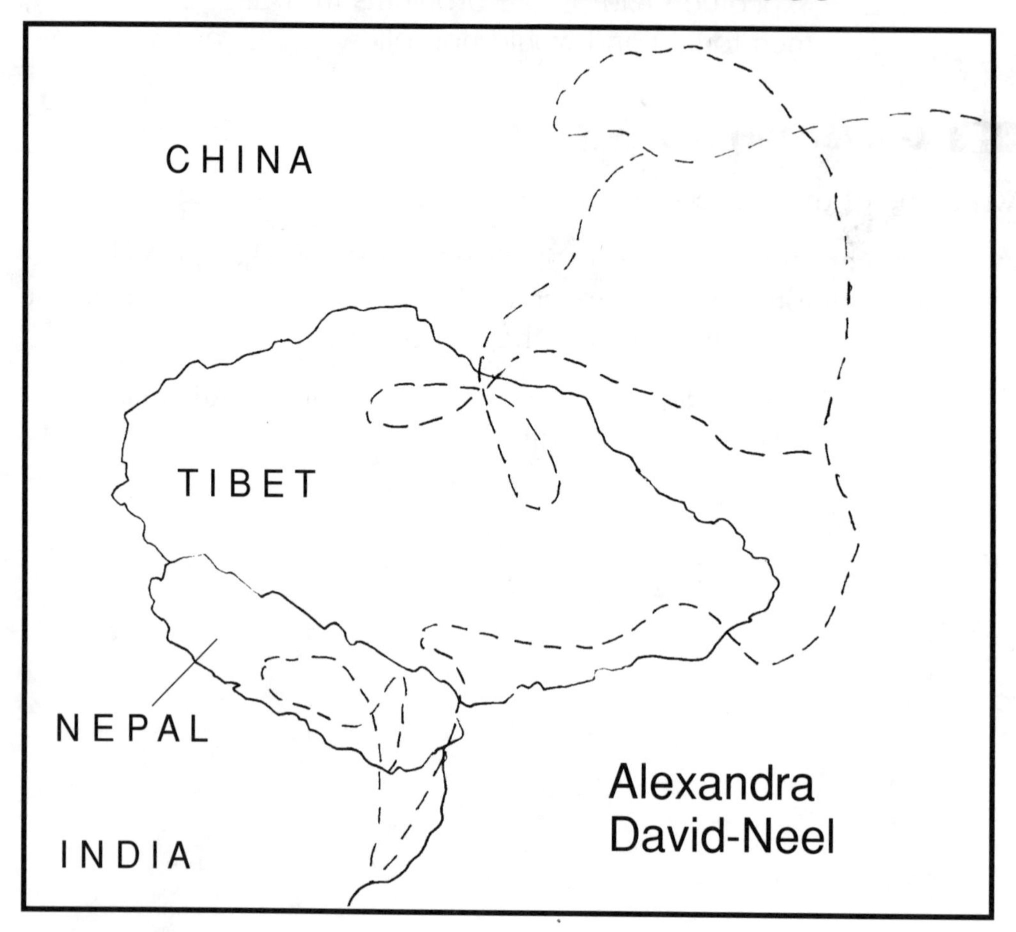

LESSON

Pre-reading Questions

1. **Are you a Buddhist, or do you know someone who is?**
2. **Do you know someone who has visited Tibet?**
3. **Where would you go if you wanted to study your religion?**

Context Clues

It is not necessary to look up every new word in the dictionary. You can often tell what the word means from the sentence it is in, or from the sentence after it. For example, the word **aborigines** in line 6 on page 3 is explained in the next sentence. What are aborigines?

Always look for this kind of sentence when you are reading. Try not to look up the word in your dictionary.

Here are some sentences from the lessons in this unit. Tell what each word in **bold** print means. Do all of the Context Clues exercises in the book this way.

1. She started working as a **journalist**, writing articles about Asia and Buddhism for English and French magazines and newspapers.
2. Scott took **ponies** (small horses) and a few dogs.
3. She helped to start **anthropology**, the study of people's customs and lives, in Africa.
4. Europeans bought elephant **ivory** and other things from Africans.
5. She met **traders** there, Europeans who bought ivory and other things from Africans and sold them things from Europe.
6. **Missionaries** went to Africa to teach Christianity.

2

Alexandra David-Neel—A French Woman in Tibet

Tibet has been a secret and **mysterious** place to the rest of the world for several centuries. It is on a high **plateau** in Asia, **surrounded** by even higher mountains, and only a few foreigners were able to cross its **borders** until recently.

> plateau: high, flat land
> borders: lines between countries

One of these foreigners was a French woman named Alexandra David-Neel (1868–1969). She traveled by herself in India, China, and Tibet. She studied the Buddhist **religion**, wrote **articles** and books about it, and collected **ancient** Buddhist books. She also became a Buddhist herself.

> ancient: very old

Alexandra always said she had an unhappy childhood. She **escaped** her unhappiness by reading books on **adventure** and travel. She ran away from school several times and even ran away to England when she was only sixteen.

> escaped: got away from

She was a singer for several years, but in 1903 she started working as a **journalist**, writing articles about Asia and Buddhism for English and French magazines and newspapers. The next year, when she was thirty-seven, she married Philippe-François Neel. It was a strange marriage. After 5 days together, they moved to different

25 cities and never lived together again. **Yet** he **supported** her all his life, and she wrote him hundreds of letters full of **details** about her travels.

but

gave her money to live on

She traveled all over Europe and North Af-
30 rica, but she went to India in 1911 to study Buddhism, and then her real travels began. She traveled in India and also in Nepal and Sikkim, the small countries north of India in the Himalaya Mountains, but her goal was Tibet. She continued
35 to study Buddhism and learned to speak Tibetan. She traveled to villages and religious centers, with only an interpreter and a few men to carry her camping **equipment**. For several months, she lived in a **cave** in Sikkim and studied Buddhism
40 and the Tibetan language. Then she **adopted** a fifteen-year-old Sikkimese boy to travel with her. He remained with her until his death at the age of fifty-five.

cave

For the next 7 years, she traveled in **remote**
45 **areas** of China. These were years of **civil war** in China, and she was often in danger. She traveled for thousands of kilometers on horseback with only a few men to help her—through desert heat, sandstorms, and the rain, snow, and **freezing**
50 **temperatures** of the colder areas.

remote areas = far from towns and cities

civil war = war between people in the same country

0° C or colder

In 1924, David-Neel was fifty-six years old. She darkened her skin and dressed as an old **beggar**. She carried only a beggar's bowl and a backpack and traveled through hot lowlands and snowy
55 mountain passes until she reached the border of Tibet. Because she spoke Tibetan so well, she was able to cross the border and reach the famous city of Lhasa without anyone knowing that she was European and **forbidden** to be there. It was
60 often freezing cold, and sometimes there wasn't enough food. Sometimes she was sick, and once she nearly died. This was the most dangerous of all

beggar

not allowed

her journeys, but she reached her goal and collected more information about Tibetan Buddhism.

65 She returned to France in 1925. She spent several years writing about her **research** and adventures and translating ancient Tibetan religious books. When she was sixty-six, she returned to China and the Tibetan border area for 70 10 years. In 1944, the Second World War reached even that remote area, and at the age of seventy-six, she walked for days, sometimes without food, until she was able to reach a place where she could fly to India and then home to France. She 75 continued writing and translating until she died, just 7 weeks before her 101st birthday.

research: search for new information

Most explorers traveled to **discover** and map new places. David-Neel went to do research on Buddhism. She said that freedom was the 80 most important thing in life for her, and like many other explorers, she lived a dangerous, exciting, free life.

A Vocabulary

Write the correct word in each blank. Use each word only once, and use capital letters if they are necessary.

civil war	temperature	freezes	border
mysterious	article	ancient	discovered
caves	journalist	remote	forbidden
equipment	adventure	beggars	plateau

1. It would be a great ________________ to travel in Tibet on horseback.
2. There is an interesting ________________ in the newspaper today about Tibet.
3. You can find ________________ asking for money in most countries.
4. When Ali got to his car, he ________________ that he had a parking ticket.
5. Some ancient North Americans lived in ________________. Others built houses.

6. Smoking is ________________ in the front rows in most airplanes.
7. When water ________________, it turns into ice.
8. Did you bring all the sports ________________ for our picnic?
9. The Himalayas are on the ________________ between China and India.
10. A ________________ collects information and then writes articles about it for magazines and newspapers.
11. The language of ________________ Egypt was different from the modern Egyptian language.
12. The United States had a ________________ between the northern and southern states from 1861 to 1865.

B Vocabulary

Remember to underline the words you don't know as you read the text, and then test yourself when you finish the lesson.

plateau	escaped	area	mysterious
details	surrounded	support	journalist
yet	research	border	religion
adopted	temperature	remote	frozen

1. It's hot today. What is the ________________?
2. Northern Siberia is ________________ from Russian cities.
3. A ________________ noise woke me up in the middle of the night.
4. Mr. and Mrs. Thompson ________________ a baby because they couldn't have any children of their own.
5. What is your ________________? Are you a Christian?
6. Most English paragraphs have a main idea and supporting ________________.
7. Parents usually ________________ their children until the children finish school. The parents pay for everything the children need.
8. Dr. Garcia is doing ________________ for space exploration.
9. Tibet is a remote place, ________________ tourists go there now.
10. A man ________________ from prison last night. He is dangerous.
11. Our house is ________________ by big trees.

12. Tibet is on a ________________ north of the Himalayas.
13. There are a lot of apartment buildings in the ________________ around the university.

C Multiple Choice

Circle the letter of the best answer. An asterisk (*) means it is an inference or opinion question, and you cannot find the answer in a sentence in the text.

1. Alexandra David-Neel went to Asia to ______.
   a. study Buddhism
   b. lead an expedition
   c. adopt a son

2. When she was a child, she read to ______.
   a. become a Buddhist
   b. escape her unhappiness
   c. learn about Europe

3. After she got married, ______.
   a. she lived in Europe with her husband for several years
   b. her husband supported her
   c. her husband traveled in Europe with her

*4. It is possible that she ______.
   a. took photographs during her travels
   b. had a car when she lived in a cave
   c. spoke Tibetan to her Indian friends

5. The place she wanted most to visit was ______.
   a. India
   b. China
   c. Tibet

6. Her travels in China were dangerous because ______.
   a. there was a civil war
   b. she was traveling on horseback
   c. she was a beggar

7. David-Neel said that ______.
   a. she wasn't afraid of danger
   b. freedom was very important to her
   c. she wanted her husband to travel with her

D Comprehension Questions

Always answer the comprehension questions with complete sentences.

1. Why is Tibet a mysterious place?
*2. Why did Alexandra run away from school?
3. What is a journalist?
4. Why was her marriage strange?
5. What did she do when she was living in a cave?
6. What does *remote areas* mean?
7. Why didn't the Tibetans know she was a foreigner?
8. What kind of work did she do after her last trip?
*9. Do you think she lived a free life? Why?

E Main Idea

What is the main idea of paragraph 3, (lines 13–17)?

1. Alexandra read books on travel and adventure.
2. Alexandra ran away from school several times.
3. Alexandra had an unhappy childhood.

F Word Forms

Choose the right word form for each sentence. Use a word from line 1 in sentence 1, and so on. Use the right verb forms and singular or plural nouns. There are blanks on the chart because there are not 4 forms for every word.

	Verb	Noun	Adjective	Adverb
1.	mystify	mystery	mysterious	mysteriously
2.	surround	surroundings		
3.	beg	beggar		
4.		religion	religious	religiously
5.		adventure	adventurous	adventurously
6.	supply	supply		
7.	equip	equipment		
8.	adopt	adoption		
9.	discover	discovery		
10.	decide	decision		decidedly

1. I saw an exciting television program last night. It was a ________________.
2. Dan drove so fast on his vacation trip that he hardly saw his ________________.
3. Small children often ________________ to go with their parents when the parents go out at night.
4. Alexandra David-Neel was a very ________________ person.
5. David-Neel was also very ________________.
6. The company was unable to ________________ most of the things we ordered.
7. The Browns are going to ________________ their truck with a telephone.
8. It is very difficult to ________________ children in the United States today.
9. Captain James Cook is famous for the ________________ of many Pacific islands.

10a. Sometimes it is difficult to make a good ________________ about a difficult problem.

10b. David-Neel was a ________________ adventurous person. There is no question about it.

G Articles

A and **an** are used to show that the noun after it is one of a group.

John Burke was **an** explorer. (He was one of all the explorers in history.)

Maria is **a** student. (She is one of all the students in the world.)

There is **an** apple in the refrigerator. (This is one of all the apples in the world.)

The is used to show that the noun is one special, particular, specific noun or nouns.

John Burke and William John Wills were **the** first explorers to cross Australia.

Maria is **the** best student in the class.

There is an apple in **the** refrigerator. (We know that we are talking about the refrigerator in our kitchen.)

Put the right article in the blanks.

1. Australia is ______ huge country.
2. ______ journalist who wrote this article is a friend of mine.
3. David-Neel was ______ journalist.
4. Please close ______ door.
5. Her office is ______ first one on the left.
6. ______ professor called you today, but I don't know who it was.
7. Who was ______ worst teacher you ever had?

H Compound Words

Compound words are common in English. They are two words put together, and the meaning of the compound word is related to the meanings of the two words. They are not like two-word verbs where the meaning is different from the meaning of each word by itself. Put these compound words in the right blanks.

horseback	sandstorm	snowstorm	keyhole
mailbox	sidewalk	doorbell	weekend

1. Barbara couldn't drive to her parents' last week because there was a bad ________________ and it was very cold.
2. Abdullah looks in his ________________ every day, and he usually finds a letter.
3. A ________________ is a place for people to walk at the side of the street.
4. When you unlock a door, you put your key in the ________________.
5. The ________________ rang, and Susan went to answer the door.
6. Did you ever go ________________ riding?

I Guided Writing

Write one of these two short compositions.

1. You are Alexandra David-Neel. Write a letter to your husband. Describe one or two of your adventures in some detail. Add your own ideas about what you saw, heard, felt, touched, or smelled.

2. Describe an adventure you had or an unusual trip you took. Use details about what you saw, heard, felt, touched, or smelled.

Vitus Bering—Across Siberia to North America

LESSON

Pre-reading Questions

1. **Have you traveled to Siberia or to Alaska? If so, tell your classmates about your journey.**
2. **What is the name of the body of water between Siberia and Alaska? (If no one in the class knows the answer, you will find it in the story.)**
3. **Which are longer in Siberia and Alaska, winters or summers?**

Context Clues

You can often guess the meaning of a word from the sentence even if the sentence doesn't explain the word exactly. For example, in this lesson, a sentence says, "They lost a lot of food when one of the ships **sank** in a storm." What could a storm do to a ship so that the food was lost? The ship probably went down into the water to the bottom of the ocean. When you can guess easily what the word means from the sentence, don't look up the word in your dictionary.

Now practice with these new words from this unit. Circle the letter of the best meaning of the **bold** word.

1. Please write your **complete** name, not just your family name.
   a. first b. whole c. first and last
2. David-Neel had to go to China first **in order to** go to Tibet.
   a. to b. by c. for
3. This book **includes** lessons on explorers, science, and medicine.
   a. has in it
   b. has complete information
   c. has only
4. On my last flight to London, there was a **delay** of 3 hours because of bad weather. I waited in an airport restaurant.
   a. danger b. line c. wait
5. After 3 weeks at sea, the sailors were happy to go **ashore** in Singapore.
   a. for the weekend b. to the land c. swimming
6. After the **decade** of 1990–1999, it will be the twenty-first century.
   a. one hundred years b. ten years c. fifty years

3

Vitus Bering—Across Siberia to North America

In 1733, the most **complete** scientific expedition in history up to that time left St. Petersburg, Russia, to explore the east coast of Siberia and discover if Asia and North America were joined. The scientists planned to report on everything: the geography, **climate**, plants, animals, and the **customs** and languages of the Siberian people.

The expedition had to cross Siberia **in order to** reach the Pacific Ocean. Vitus Bering, the leader of the whole expedition, left St. Petersburg with almost 600 people. The group **included** a few scientists, **skilled** workers of all kinds, soldiers, and sailors. Alexei Chirikov left later with most of the scientists and tons of supplies.

in order to: to
included: had in it

It took 7 years for Bering's and Chirikov's groups to cross Siberia. They traveled mostly in flat-bottomed boats on the rivers. Bering's group spent a year in Tobolsk, where they built a ship and explored the Ob River. They continued to Yakutsk, where they spent 4 years. Yakutsk was only a small village, so they had to build their own buildings because there were so many people in the expedition. They also built boats and explored the Lena River. Then they moved on to Okhotsk on the eastern coast. It took 2 more

years to build ships so they could explore and map the east coast.

Bering made careful plans, but there were always problems. For example, they lost a lot of their food when one of the ships **sank** in a storm. But finally, their 2 ships started for North America. They had only one summer instead of 2 years for their explorations because of the many problems and **delays**. And summers are short in the North.

sank: went to the bottom of the ocean

There was more bad luck. There were storms, and the two ships were **separated**, but at last the sailors on Bering's ship saw mountains a short **distance** across the sea. This proved that North America and Asia were two separate continents.

separated: moved apart

Their problems continued. Their water supply was low, but when the men went **ashore** in Alaska, they got water that was a little salty. Many of the men were sick from **scurvy**, a disease caused by the **lack** of **vitamin** C. When they drank the salty water, they became even sicker. Then they started dying, one after another.

lack: not enough of or none

As the ship sailed south, back toward Okhotsk, it became lost in storms. Finally, a storm drove it onto a small island, and the men knew their ship could not sail again. They were in a place with no trees, but there were birds and animals for food, and **fresh** water to drink. However, it was too late for many of them. Men continued to die from scurvy, and on December 8, 1741, Bering died and was **buried** on the island that is now named for him. When spring came, the few remaining men were able to build a small ship from the wood in the old one and leave the island.

By this time, the Russian government had lost interest in the North Pacific. Bering's reports were sent back to St. Petersburg and forgotten. **Decades** later, people **realized** that Bering was

Decades: one decade = 10 years

a great explorer. His expedition **gathered** important scientific information about the interior of Siberia, made maps of the eastern coast, and
70 discovered a new part of North America. Today we have the Bering Sea between Siberia and Alaska to **remind us** of the leader of this great scientific expedition.

make us remember

A Vocabulary

complete	realize	included	delay
distance	bury	gather	history
remind	sink	separate	lack

1. They could see something in the ________________, but they couldn't tell what it was.
2. Did you study the ________________ of your country in school?
3. Mr. and Mrs. Baker drive to work in ________________ cars because they work in different places.
4. Please ________________ me to buy some bread, or I might forget.
5. In some restaurants, the waiter's or waitress's tip is ________________ in the bill. In others, you leave it separately.
6. You should do the ________________ lesson for tomorrow's homework. Do all the exercises.
7. There will be a short ________________ while the chemistry professor gets the equipment ready.
8. He didn't ________________ what time it was, and he got to class late.
9. Wood doesn't ________________ in water. Rocks do.
10. Burke's expedition failed partly because of his ________________ of experience in the Australian outback.

B Vocabulary

climate	in order to	bury	gathered
custom	ashore	fresh	skilled
complete	decade	vitamin	scurvy

1. Ali is studying English ________________ go to an American university.
2. In many countries, it is the ________________ to ________________ people when they die.
3. Ann ________________ up her books and papers and left the library.
4. ________________, caused by the lack of vitamin C, was a problem on ships on long trips.
5. North Africa has a desert ________________.
6. A century is 100 years. A ________________ is 10.
7. Electricians and mechanics are ________________ workers.
8. After a half hour in the water, the children swam ________________ and dried off.
9. People cannot drink seawater. They need ________________ water.
10. ________________ C is found in oranges.

C Vocabulary Review: Definitions

Match the words with their meaning. Write the letter and the definition from the second column in the correct blank.

1. hemisphere ________________	a. not fight
2. border ________________	b. find
3. forbidden ________________	c. high, flat land
4. get along ________________	d. inside
5. research ________________	e. half of the earth
6. plateau ________________	f. not allowed
7. discover ________________	g. 100 years
8. ancient ________________	h. writer for magazines
9. turn into ________________	i. search for new information
10. journalist ________________	j. very old
	k. become
	l. line between two countries

D True/False/Not Enough Information

Write **T** if the sentence is true, **F** if it is false, and **NI** if there is not enough information in the text. Change the false sentences to make them true, or explain why they are false. Do all of the **True/False** exercises in the lessons this way.

_______ 1. Bering left St. Petersburg ahead of Chirikov.
_______ 2. It took them 7 years to cross Siberia because they were traveling on horseback.
_______ 3. Vitus Bering was from St. Petersburg.
_______ 4. Bering spent 2 years exploring the east coast of Siberia.
_______ *5. Bering's and Burke's expeditions were similar.
_______ 6. Bering's men found Eskimos in Alaska.
_______ 7. Scurvy is caused by a lack of vitamin C.
_______ 8. Alaska belonged to the United States at the time of Bering's expedition.

E Comprehension Questions

Paraphrase your answers. That means try to answer the comprehension questions in your own words instead of using the exact words from the text.

1. Why was this called a scientific expedition?
2. What did the men on the expedition do in Tobolsk?
3. Where did they stay longer, in Tobolsk or Yakutsk?
*4. Why did the expedition have to build boats?
5. How did the two ships get separated in the Pacific Ocean?
6. Why did the men on the island continue to die even when they had food and water?
*7. Is scurvy a problem on ships today? Why or why not?
*8. When Bering's expedition returned to St. Petersburg, were they welcomed as national heroes? Why or why not?

F Main Idea

What is the main idea of paragraph 3 (lines 16–28)?

1. It took 7 years to cross Siberia.
2. The expedition explored two rivers.
3. The expedition built their own village in Yakutsk.

G Reading

How carefully should you read? How fast should you read? These questions have different answers. Sometimes you have to read slowly and carefully. At other times, you read fast, and at still other times, you read at a regular speed.

How would you read these things? Use these answers:
a. slowly and carefully b. at a regular speed c. fast
(Students may have different answers.)

1. a letter from your parents
2. the text of these lessons
3. the homework for a difficult science class
4. the newspaper
5. a magazine article on an interesting person
6. an exciting mystery story

Some students like to read the whole text quickly for the general idea. Others like to start at the beginning and read each sentence carefully. You can choose the best way for you to start reading a lesson. After that, you probably need to read the lesson two or three times. When you come to a word you don't know, read the sentence again, or even three times, to help you remember the word. It is never necessary to memorize sentences or paragraphs. That is not the way to study reading.

If the text is very difficult for you, read the first paragraph two or three times, then the second, and so on. Then read the whole text from beginning to end. Then you might want to read it all again.

You will probably want to read the complete text again after you have finished the whole lesson. Then test yourself on the vocabulary words that you underlined when you first read the text and learn the words you don't know.

H Word Forms: Verbs

How do you know which form of a word to use? This information will help you.

Every sentence must have a verb. There are often clues that tell you what form of the verb to use.

Put the right verb forms in these blanks. Explain why you chose each form.

(lead)	1. Did Bering ________________ an expedition across Siberia?
(leave)	2. The expedition ________________ St. Petersburg in 1733.
(study)	3. Bob is ________________ about explorers.
(learn)	4. Nadia has ________________ a lot of words this week.
(help)	5. Can you ________________ me with this exercise?
(give)	6. The teacher ________________ a lot of homework every day.
(sleep)	7. Mr. Gorder was ________________ at midnight last night.
(travel)	8. They are going to ________________ in Europe next summer.

I Prepositions

Prepositions are difficult. The best way to learn how to use the right preposition is by practicing. Write the prepositions in these sentences from the text.

1. ______ 1733, the most complete scientific expedition in history ______ ______ that time left St. Petersburg.
2. The scientists planned to report ______ everything.
3. The expedition had to cross Siberia ______ order ______ reach the Pacific Ocean.
4. Vitus Bering, the leader ______ the expedition, left St. Petersburg ______ almost 600 people.
5. They traveled mostly ______ flat-bottomed boats ______ the rivers.

6. They had only one summer instead ______ 2 years ______ their explorations because ______ the many problems and delays.
7. At last, the sailors ______ Bering's ship saw mountains a short distance ______ the sea.
8. They were ______ a place ______ no trees, but there were birds and animals ______ food.
9. ______ this time, the Russian government had lost interest ______ the North Pacific.
10. It discovered a new part ______ North America.

J Guided Writing

Write one of these two short compositions.

1. You are one of the men who left the island in the spring of 1742. Tell what happened to you during the decade from 1733 to 1743. Give a few details.

2. The reading does not say what happened to the people on Chirikov's ship after the two ships were separated. What do you think happened to them? Describe a few of their adventures.

Robert Scott—A Race to the South Pole

LESSON

Pre-reading Questions

1. **On which continent do we find the South Pole?**
2. **Why are people (instead of animals) pulling the sled? What do you think is on the sled?**
3. **Why are there no trees in the picture?**

Context Clues

The words in the Context Clues exercises are always words in this lesson. Circle the letter of the best meaning of the **bold** word.

1. Isamu's English is not very good. He **frequently** makes mistakes.
   a. quickly b. often c. never
2. Oil, gas, and wood are kinds of **fuel**.
   a. something to burn for heat
   b. something to make cars go
   c. something to build ships from
3. David-Neel walked for days when she was seventy-six years old. She was often **exhausted**.
   a. very hungry b. very tired c. very old
4. Jean was in an automobile accident and **injured** her leg.
   a. hurt b. stepped on c. stood on
5. **At times** David-Neel became sick from the food she ate.
   a. usually b. sometimes c. at different hours
6. Burke's expedition had **terrible** problems, and several men died.
   a. large b. interesting c. very bad
7. We know about Burke's expedition because he wrote in a **diary** every day. The search party found it.
   a. a notebook about what happened every day
   b. a cassette recording about what happened every day
   c. a book about a person's life

Robert Scott—A Race to the South Pole

Roald Amundsen, a Norwegian, was the first person to reach the South Pole. Robert Scott, who was English, arrived at the South Pole a month after Amundsen and died on the return 5 journey to his ship. Yet, strangely enough, Scott became a hero, but Amundsen did not.

Captain Robert Scott (1868–1912) was an officer in the English navy. He led an expedition to Antarctica in 1901–1904 for a British scientific 10 **organization** called the Royal Geographical Society. His group traveled farther south than anyone else had ever done, and he gathered information on rocks, weather, and climate, and made maps. When he returned to England, he was a 15 national hero.

A few years later, he decided to organize another expedition. He said he wanted to make a complete scientific study of Antarctica, but he really wanted to be the first person at the South 20 Pole. He took three doctors, several scientists, and other men with him.

They sailed on a ship named the *Terra Nova* in June 1910, but when they reached Australia, they learned that Amundsen was also on his way 25 to the Pole.

Amundsen and Scott were very different from **each other** and made very different plans. Amundsen planned everything very carefully. He took **sleds** and dog teams as the great Arctic explorers did. Scott took **ponies** (small horses) and a few dogs, but he planned to have his men pull the sleds themselves for most of the trip. On other expeditions, as some dogs became weak, the men killed them for food for themselves and the other dogs. Amundsen did this too, and it helped him reach the Pole, but later people called him "dog eater." Scott would not eat dogs, and this was one reason he died on this expedition.

There were other differences between the two expeditions. Amundsen sailed 100 kilometers closer to the Pole than Scott did. Scott also had the bad luck of having very bad weather—days of **blizzards** and strong winds. It was often −40° C (minus 40 degrees Celsius).

storms with wind and snow

Scott and his men built a building near the ocean's edge as their base camp and spent the winter there. They used sleds and ponies to carry a ton of supplies farther **inland** to a place that they named the One Ton Depot. When spring came, a few of the men started ahead of the others with motorized sleds to leave supplies along the way. However, after only a few days, the sleds **broke down** and the men had to pull them.

toward the interior

A few days later, Scott started for the South Pole with a few men. The whole journey was very difficult. Scott and his men either walked through deep snow or skied over ice and uneven ground. The climate was too difficult for the ponies, and they all died. There were **frequent** snowstorms. Sometimes the men couldn't leave their **tents** for several days because of blizzards.

often

When Scott was 260 kilometers from the Pole, he sent all but four men back to the base

camp. This was probably his most **serious** mis-
65 take. He had a tent big enough for 4 people and only enough food and **fuel** for 4, but now there were 5. Also, one man had left his skis behind with some of the supplies. He had to walk in the snow, and this slowed down the whole group.

70 On January 17, 1912, Scott and his men reached the Pole, only to find a tent and the Norwegian flag. They were not the first people to reach the South Pole. They had lost the race.

The next day, they started the 1300-
75 kilometer journey back to their base camp, pulling their heavy sleds full of supplies. The trip back was worse than the trip on the way to the Pole. They became weak from hunger. **At times** the whiteness everywhere made them **blind**. Their
80 fingers and toes began to freeze, and two of the men fell and **injured** themselves. They never had enough fuel to keep warm in their tent. They became **exhausted**, and it was more and more difficult to pull the sleds.

sometimes

unable to see

hurt

very tired

85 Finally, one man died. Then another became so weak that he knew he was endangering the lives of the others. One night he left the tent and never returned. He walked out into the blizzard to die instead of holding back the other three.

90 Every day Scott described the **terrible** journey in his **diary**. On March 21, the three remaining men were only 20 kilometers from the One Ton Depot, but another blizzard kept them in their tent. On March 29, they were still unable to
95 leave their tent. On that day, Scott wrote his last words in his diary.

A search party found the three bodies 8 months later. They also found Scott's diary, excellent photographs of the expedition, and letters
100 to take back to England. The search party left the frozen bodies where they found them.

Today the building at the base camp is still there. Inside there are supplies, furniture, and things that belonged to the men. They are left
105 just the way they were when Scott's expedition was there. New Zealand takes care of the building and its contents.

Robert Scott's name lives on as a great explorer of Antarctica, the last part of the earth that
110 people explored. He was not the first to reach the South Pole, and he and his men died because of his bad planning, but he is remembered as one of the great heroes of exploration.

A Vocabulary

organization	each other	sleds	inland
pony	blizzard	break down	exhausted
blind	frequent	fuel	at times

1. A ________________ is a storm with wind and snow.
2. Scott and his men slept close to ________________ in a small tent.
3. A ________________ is a small horse, not a young horse.
4. People who grow up near the sea are often unhappy if they have to move ________________.
5. A ________________ person cannot see.
6. There are ________________ storms in the Bering Sea in winter. In summer there are not as many.
7. Most American universities have a foreign student ____________. All students are welcome.
8. ________________ Burke rode horseback. At other times, he walked.
9. People need ________________ to cook and to heat their homes.
10. Children in Canada like to ride downhill on their ____________.

B Vocabulary

tent	terrible	serious	exhausted
broke down	fuel	injured	diary

1. We got home very late because our car ________________.
2. Tom ________________ himself at work and had to go to the hospital.
3. Some students are very ________________ about learning English.
4. Some people like to write in a ________________ every day about the things they do and think.
5. Last summer our family went camping in the mountains. We slept in a ________________.
6. Ali stayed up all night to study for a test. He was ________________ in the morning.
7. There was a ________________ fire in an old apartment building, and 10 people died.

C Vocabulary Review: Antonyms

Match the words with their opposites.

1. huge ________________	a. in back of
2. experienced ________________	b. swamp
3. get along ________________	c. modern
4. forbid ________________	d. fight
5. complete ________________	e. together
6. include ________________	f. incomplete
7. ahead of ________________	g. leave out
8. separated ________________	h. inexperienced
9. interior ________________	i. escape
10. lack ________________	j. allow
11. ancient ________________	k. small
	l. exterior
	m. have

D Multiple Choice

1. The first person to reach the South Pole was ______.
   a. English b. French c. Norwegian

2. Scott was mainly interested in ______.
   a. being the first person at the South Pole
   b. collecting information about the rocks in Antarctica
   c. learning about the weather and climate in Antarctica

*3. Amundsen's expedition ate dogs because ______.
   a. this is a custom in Norway
   b. it was a way for the men to have fresh meat
   c. there was no other food

*4. Scott's expedition had to travel ______.
   a. a shorter distance than Amundsen's
   b. the same distance as Amundsen's
   c. farther than Amundsen's

*5. January is a ______ month in Antarctica.
   a. summer b. fall c. winter

6. Scott's trip to the Pole was difficult. The trip back was ______.
   a. more difficult
   b. about the same
   c. much easier

*7. Scott and his men became exhausted because ______.
   a. they didn't have enough fuel and they could never get warm
   b. the sun on the snow blinded them
   c. they didn't have enough food and had to pull the heavy sleds

8. We know the details about Scott's expedition because______.
   a. he sent reports back to the English government
   b. he kept a diary, and the search party found it
   c. he wrote detailed letters back to England

E Comprehension Questions

*1. Scott and Burke led expeditions in very different climates. What was similar about their expeditions?
2. Explain one serious mistake that Scott made.
*3. Why did Scott travel from his base camp to the Pole in January?
4. Why did one man walk out of the tent into the blizzard and not return?
5. Why was it difficult for the men to pull the sleds on the trip back from the Pole?
6. Why couldn't the three men travel the last 20 kilometers to the One Ton Depot?
*7. Was Scott a hero of exploration? Give a reason for your answer.

F Main Idea

What is the main idea of paragraph 7 (lines 45–53)?

1. moving supplies inland
2. getting ready to ski to the South Pole
3. bad luck with motorized sleds

G Word Forms: Nouns

There are three places in a sentence that always have a noun (or a pronoun): the subject, the object of a verb, and the object of a preposition.

subject	verb	object of the verb	object of a preposition
David-Neel	rode	a **horse**	to **Tibet**.
The **expedition**	took	**food**	for the **animals**.
A **storm**	drove	the **ship**	onto an **island**.

The subject is usually at the beginning of a sentence. The object of the verb is usually right after the verb. It answers the question, "What?" The object of a preposition comes after the preposition.

There might be adjectives and other words to describe these nouns.

> **David-Neel** rode a large black **horse** to **Tibet**.
> The large scientific **expedition** took a lot of **food** for the **animals**.
> A bad **storm** drove the large sailing **ship** onto a small **island**.

Write the correct word forms in the blanks. Use a word from line 1 in sentence 1, and so on. Use the right verb forms and singular or plural nouns. There are blanks on the chart because there are not four forms for every word.

Verb	Noun	Adjective	Adverb
1. include	inclusion	inclusive	inclusively
2. separate	separation	separate	separately
3. bury	burial	burial	
4. realize	realization		
5. remind	reminder		
6. inform	information	(un)informative	(un)informatively
7. organize	organization	organizational	organizationally
8. injure	injury	injurious	injuriously

1. Did you ________________ a description of your dormitory when you wrote to your family?

2a. Amadou's ________________ from his family is difficult for him, but he wants to study at a foreign university.

2b. Write your two compositions on ________________ pieces of paper. Do them ________________.

3. Mr. Byrd died yesterday, and they are going to ________________ him tomorrow. His ________________ is tomorrow.

4. After Ms. Cook got home, she ________________ she had forgotten to mail her letters.

5. Ms. Barber put a ________________ on the refrigerator for her children to do their homework.

6. Kumiko asked the teacher for ________________ about the city buses. The teacher gave her a schedule that was very ________________.

7a. An ________________ in Melbourne chose Burke to lead an expedition across Australia.

7b. The first meeting of the new club will be an
_________________ meeting.

8. Chris was in an accident, but luckily he didn't receive any
_________________.

H Two-Word Verbs

Learn these two-word verbs and then fill in the blanks with the right words. Use the correct verb form. Do all of the two-word verb exercises in the book this way.

run out of —use up, not have any more
work out —exercise
slow down—go more slowly
speed up —go faster
live on —have enough money for necessities

1. Cars have to _________________ when they enter a city. When they leave the city, they can _________________ again.
2. A lot of people like to go to a gymnasium and _________________. This exercise is good for them.
3. The Lopez family adopted two children. Now they can't _________________ the money Mr. Lopez gets for working.
4. Scott's men were hungry because they had almost _________________ food.

I Finding the Reason

Here are some sentences about the explorers you have read about. Give a reason for each statement. The first one is done for you.

	Statement	**Reason**
1.	Scott and his men were cold all the time.	They didn't have enough fuel.
2.	Scott went to the South Pole.	
3.	David-Neel studied Tibetan in India.	
4.	Bering's expedition lost a lot of its food.	
5.	Bering took scientists with him.	

6. Burke died on his expedition.
7. Burke took camels on his expedition.
8. The world knows about Burke's and Scott's expeditions.

J Guided Writing

Write one of these two short compositions.

1. You are going to lead a journey to the South Pole. What will you do differently from the way Scott did it?

2. You are in the tent with Scott in March 1912. Write a message in your diary.

Mary Kingsley—Victorian Explorer

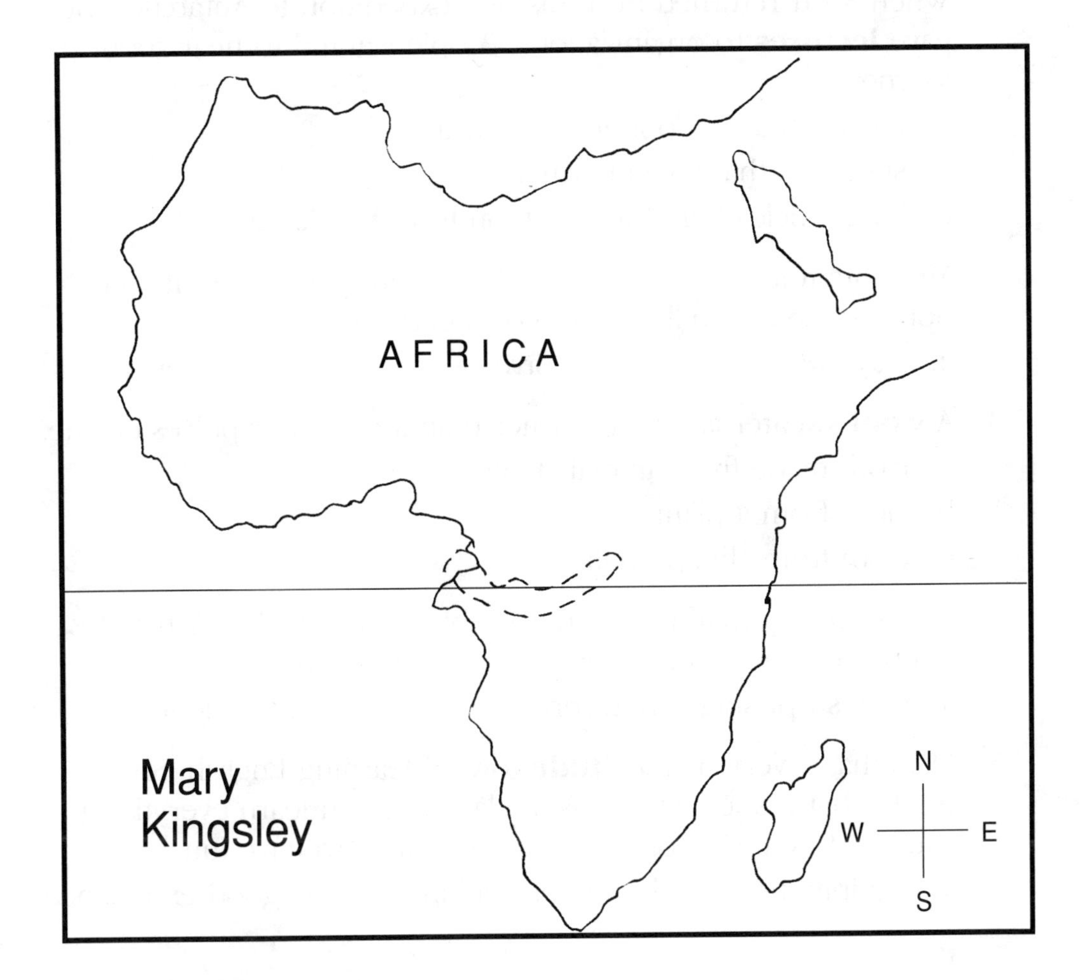

LESSON

Pre-reading Questions

1. **Did Mary Kingsley travel north or south of the equator?**
2. **Through which modern-day African countries did she travel?**
3. **What does "Victorian" mean?**

Context Clues

Circle the letter of the best meaning of the **bold** word.

1. When Scott returned from his first expedition to Antarctica, he gave **lectures** to organizations. People wanted to hear about his journey.
   a. movies that he took in Antarctica
   b. speeches that give information
   c. long articles full of information from his diaries

2. Mr. Mora told his son, "Stop fighting with your sister. If you don't **behave**, you'll have to go to bed right now."
   a. stay awake   b. act correctly   c. slow down

3. A **wool** sweater is much warmer than a cotton or polyester one.
   a. cloth made from animal skin
   b. cloth from a plant
   c. cloth from sheep's hair

4. It is **amazing** that a woman was able to travel all over the interior of China and Tibet by herself at that time.
   a. very surprising   b. terrible   c. frequent

5. Maria has a very bad **attitude** toward learning English. She thinks that if she just listens in class, she can learn everything she needs. Outside of class, she just wants to have fun.
   a. equipment   b. way of thinking   c. good experience

5

Mary Kingsley— Victorian Explorer

Mary Kingsley spent eighteen months between 1893 and 1895 exploring West Africa. The two books she wrote and the **lectures** she gave back in England about her travels helped to change the way Europeans thought about their African **colonies**. Kingsley also helped to start **anthropology**, the study of people's customs and lives, of Africa. We must understand something about English life at that time in order to understand how **amazing** this was.

lectures: educational speeches
amazing: very surprising

Mary Kingsley was born near London in 1862 and grew up while Victoria was queen of England. At that time, women were expected to stay at home, take care of their husbands and children, and **behave** like ladies.

Mary's father was a doctor, and her mother was his cook. The parents got married only 4 days before Mary was born. Her father spent most of his time traveling in far-off countries, and he hardly ever came home. Her mother was never well, and she spent her life in her bedroom with all the curtains closed. Of course, Mary had to take care of her, so Mary never married. She never went to school either; she had to **educate** herself.

When both her parents died in 1892, Mary took the money they left her and went to visit the Canary Islands off the coast of West Africa. She met **traders** there, Europeans who bought **rub-**
30 **ber**, elephant **ivory**, and other **products** from Africans and sold them things from Europe. She returned to England and studied to do useful scientific work in West Africa. During her first trip of 6 months back to West Africa and her second
35 one of more than a year, she collected fish for the British Museum. Much more important, she gathered information about African customs, law, and religion.

European men had been exploring Africa for
40 years. Each explorer took large amounts of equipment, food, and other supplies and needed many Africans to carry them. The Europeans had guns and used them when there was trouble. Kingsley traveled with only six Africans to help her. She
45 slept in village houses and ate what the Africans ate. She had a gun, but she never shot anyone. She always wore a white cotton blouse and a long **wool** skirt. She was usually the first white woman the villagers had ever seen, but they **accepted**
50 her as a friend because of the way she traveled. She was able to ask them all kinds of questions about their lives, and later she wrote detailed scientific descriptions of African customs. She also wrote beautiful descriptions of the slow-
55 moving rivers, the sounds of the African night, and the beauty of the African forest.

At that time, there were three groups of Europeans in Africa. These were the traders, the people working for the colonial governments,
60 and the **missionaries** who went to Africa to teach Christianity. They all believed that Europeans were **superior** to other people. They believed either that Africans were wild or that they

better than

were **childlike**. The English missionaries believed Africans and Europeans were brothers because they were all God's children, but they also believed that Africans were **inferior** because they were not Christians. The missionaries thought that the Africans' false religion made them live inferior lives. They thought that if Africans started wearing European clothes, learned English, forgot their old ways, and became Christians, they could become better people. The other Europeans believed that Africans were inferior and less intelligent than white people.

As Mary Kingsley gathered information about African customs, she learned that their religion was the center of their lives. Their religion and customs, even the ones that seemed very strange to Europeans, all fit together in a **logical** way. She believed that if Europeans tried to change African religion or any of their customs, the Africans' lives would be worse than before. However, she also believed that Africans could not learn **technology** and could never move into the modern world. As she wrote and lectured about her ideas, the people working in the colonial governments learned from her, and the governments became better.

When Kingsley reached a village, she usually said, "It's only me." She said it so often that villagers started calling her "Only Me" because they thought it was her name. She was European, so the Africans **treated** her like a European and not like a woman. She had much more freedom than she had when she was at home in England.

In 1900 Kingsley went to South Africa to help in the hospitals during the Boer War, but she planned to return to West Africa. However, in a short time, she became sick and died at the age of thirty-seven. She was buried at sea.

Mary Kingsley was a Victorian woman. She became an explorer, geographer, anthropologist, and author. Today it is not easy for anyone to be
105 even one of these things. In Kingsley's time, it was almost impossible, especially for a woman, but she was all of them. Her books started a change in West African history because they helped change the **attitudes** of the Europeans toward
110 the Africans in their colonies. Her great knowledge of African customs helped start the anthropological study of Africa. She was an amazing person.

A Vocabulary

products	educated	anthropology	colony
lecture	ivory	missionary	behave
childlike	superior	treats	inferior

1. Mona is the best student in the class. She is ________________ to all the other students. They are ________________ to her.
2. Pierre is Canadian, but he didn't go to school in Canada. He was ________________ in France.
3. Professor Allen will give a ________________ today about his research on fish that live in caves.
4. A ________________ tries to get people to change their religion.
5. Some people are born with inferior intelligence. They are ________________ all their lives. They never act like grown-ups.
6. Japan produces cars, television sets, computers, and other ________________.
7. Carlos always ________________ older people politely.
8. People on Réunion, an island off the east coast of Africa, speak French because Réunion is a French ________________.
9. Susan is going to study ________________.

B Vocabulary

behave	trade	accept	rubber
wool	ivory	attitude	technology
amazing	product	anthropology	logical

1. The twentieth century is the age of ________________. We have computers and other amazing machines.
2. Farmers use sheep for their meat and ________________ in New Zealand, Europe, and other areas of the world.
3. When we study the history of the world, the importance of ________________ between countries is clear.
4. Now it is illegal to kill elephants for their ________________.
5. Isamu says the reading book is too easy for him, so he never studies. Yet he always gets bad grades. This is not ________________ thinking. If he changes his ________________, he can get good grades.
6. Sometimes children ________________ badly in school.
7. ________________ comes from trees and is used to make tires for cars and trucks.
8. It is ________________ that today people in some remote areas know about the rest of the world.
9. When you live in another country, you have to ________________ the people and the customs there. You cannot change them.

C Vocabulary Review

beggar	surrounded	temperature	civil war
delayed	in order to	sink	ashore
decade	organization	tent	terrible

1. The soldiers ________________ the building so no one could escape.
2. Every year ships ________________ in storms.
3. The snowstorm ________________ us 3 hours because we had to drive very slowly.
4. A ________________ asks people for money or food.
5. OPEC means the ________________ of Petroleum Exporting Countries.
6. Did you ever sleep outdoors in a ________________?

7. There has been a ________________ in Somalia for several years. Different groups of Somalis are fighting among themselves.
8. Sometimes the summer ________________ in Antarctica is −40°C.
9. A ________________ forest fire burned thousands of hectares of trees.
10. A ________________ is 10 years.

D True/False/Not Enough Information

_______ 1. Mary Kingsley spent a total of 2 years exploring in West Africa.
_______ 2. Mary had to educate herself.
_______ 3. Traders buy and sell things.
_______ *4. European explorers sometimes shot Africans.
_______ *5. A long wool skirt and white blouse are good clothes for exploring in West Africa.
_______ 6. Kingsley took a lot of equipment with her because she was doing scientific research on fish.
_______ *7. English missionaries believed that all people are God's children.
_______ 8. The West African religion was the center of all their customs.
_______ 9. Kingsley believed that Africans could not learn technology.
_______ 10. Kingsley became sick and died in West Africa.

E Comprehension Questions

1. What was a woman's life like in Victorian England?
2. How did Mary Kingsley tell others about her research in Africa?
3. Why didn't she go to school?
4. Where did she get the money to go to the Canary Islands?
5. What are traders?
6. What are missionaries?
7. What is a colony?
8. How were Kingsley's expeditions different from the expeditions of European men?
9. How did Kingsley do her research?

10. What did Kingsley believe about trying to change African customs?
11. How did her books help change West African history?

F Main Idea

What is the main idea of paragraph 9 (lines 97–101)?

1. Kingsley worked in a hospital in South Africa.
2. Kingsley died in South Africa in 1900.
3. Kingsley was buried at sea.

G Scanning

When you want to find just one detail in a text, it is not necessary to read carefully. You **scan instead; that is, you look as quickly as possible until you find the information.**

Find these answers by scanning. Write short answers (not complete sentences). Write the number of the line where you found each answer.

1. When was Mary Kingsley born?
2. What did she wear on her expeditions?
3. What did Africans call her?
4. How old was she when she died?
5. When did her parents die?
6. Why did missionaries go to Africa?
7. Who was queen when Kingsley was born?
8. What was the name of the war in South Africa in 1900?
9. Kingsley was an explorer. What else was she?

H Word Forms: Nouns

These are some common noun suffixes:

-er, -ar, -or: reminder, beggar, advisor
-ist: scientist
-ment: equipment
-ion, -sion, -tion, -ation: religion, decision, separation, realization
-y: discovery
-ity: electricity
-ness: happiness
-ance: acceptance

Put the right form of the word in each sentence. There are blanks on the chart because there are not 4 forms for every word.

	Verb	Noun	Adjective	Adverb
1.	trade	trade trader		
2.	produce	product production	(un)productive	(un)productively
3.	accept	acceptance	(un)acceptable	(un)acceptably
4.	(mis)behave	(mis)behavior		
5.	educate	education	(un)educated	
6.	treat	treatment		
7.	amaze	amazement	amazing	amazingly
8.	colonize	colony colonist	colonial	

1. Japan and Saudi Arabia ________________ with each other.
2a. Mexico's ________________ of oil is higher this year than last.
2b. It is ________________ to translate each lesson into your language. This is not a good way to study English.
3. Your homework is not ________________ because the teacher can't read it.
4. The children are on their good ________________ because they are going to a party.
5. ________________ is very important for everyone.
6. The boss ________________ Ann very badly during the meeting.
7. Ali looked with ________________ at the tall buildings in New York. They are ________________ high.
8. France ________________ North Africa in the nineteenth century.

I Prepositions

Write the correct prepositions in the blanks.

1. Anthropology is the study ______ people's customs and lives.
2. We must understand something ______ English life ______ that time ______ order ______ understand how amazing this was.

3. ______ that time, women were expected to stay ______ home, take care ______ their husbands and children, and behave like ladies.
4. Her mother spent her life ______ her bedroom ______ all the curtains closed.
5. Mary took the money they left her and went to visit the Canary Islands ______ the coast ______ West Africa.
6. She studied to do useful work ______ West Africa.
7. ______ her first trip ______ 6 months and her second one ______ eighteen months, she collected fish ______ the British Museum.
8. They accepted her as a friend because ______ the way she traveled.
9. They all believed that Europeans were superior ______ other people.

J Articles: The

Some geographical locations include **the in the name.**

1. Certain countries (Note: Most countries do *not* include **the** in the name.):
   the United States of America, or the United States, or the U.S.A., or the U.S.
   the United Arab Emirates
   the United Kingdom
   the Philippines
   the Netherlands
2. Major points on the earth:
   the North Pole
   the South Pole
   the equator
3. Plurals of islands, lakes, and mountains:
   the Canary Islands
   the Great Lakes
   the Himalaya Mountains
4. Oceans, seas, rivers, canals, deserts:
   the Pacific Ocean
   the Bering Sea
   the Mississippi River
   the Suez Canal
   the Sahara Desert

5. Continents, most geographical areas, most countries, and single islands, lakes, and mountains do not have **the** in the name.
   Asia
   Western Europe, but **the Middle East**
   England
   Bering Island
   Lake Geneva
   Mount Everest

Write **the** in the blanks if it is necessary.

1. ______ Panama Canal joins ______ Atlantic Ocean and ______ Pacific Ocean.
2. This canal used to belong to ______ United States.
3. ______ Kuwait is near ______ United Arab Emirates and ______ Saudi Arabia.
4. ______ Germany, ______ Belgium, and ______ Netherlands are in ______ Europe.
5. ______ Lake Geneva is in ______ Switzerland.
6. Where are ______ Madeira Islands?
7. ______ Jordan is in ______ Middle East.
8. ______ Amazon River is in ______ South America.

K Guided Writing

Write one of these two short compositions.

1. In what ways do you agree with Mary Kingsley's opinions of Africans? In what ways do you disagree? Explain.

2. Did any group of people ever come to your country or to your part of the world with the attitude that people in your country were inferior to them? Describe what happened to the people in your country and to the others. How do you feel about what happened?

World Issues

Our responsibility is to protect the Earth for a million years.
—Robert Hunter, environmentalist

World Population Growth

LESSON

Pre-reading Questions

1. **How many people live in your country? In your city?**
2. **Think of your city with twice as many people as it has now. How are things different?**
3. **Do you want to have any children? How many? Why?**

Context Clues

1. What is the answer when you add these **figures**: 739, 526, and 43?

   a. numbers   b. kilometers   c. kilos

2. Petroleum, iron, rich farmland, and coal for making electricity are all **natural resources**.

   a. anything people can use
   b. anything people make
   c. anything from nature that people can use

3. What is the best **method** to learn a language?

   a. lesson   b. way   c. composition

4. When two crowded trains run into each other, this is a **disaster**. When heavy rains cause a river to flood a village, this is also a **disaster**.

   a. anything terrible caused by people
   b. anything terrible caused by nature
   c. anything terrible that happens

5. A **shortage** of food in a poor country can cause people to die of hunger.

   a. poor farmland
   b. not enough
   c. plants that are not tall enough

6. A few tickets for the basketball game are still **available**, but you should buy one as soon as possible before they are all sold out.

   a. You can get one.
   b. They didn't make any.
   c. These tickets are too expensive.

7. When we meet a group of people from another country, it is easy to think that they are all alike; that they look similar and think in the same way. But this is not true. Each one is really an **individual**.

   a. part of a group
   b. a different, separate person
   c. similar to the other people in the family

8. The teacher **distributed** the tests and the students started working on them.
   a. collected
   b. corrected
   c. passed out

1

World Population Growth

Is the world **overpopulated**? How many people can the earth support? Should countries try to **limit** their **population**? These are serious questions that governments, **international** organizations, and **individuals** must think about.

population: number of people in an area

individual = 1 person

The population of the world has been **increasing** faster and faster. In 10,000 B.C., there were probably only 10 million people. In A.D. 1, there were 300 million. It took 1750 years for the population to reach 625 million, a little more than double the A.D. 1 **figure**. In 1850, only 100 years later, the population had nearly doubled again, with a figure of 1130 million. In 1950, the figure had more than doubled to reach 2510 million. In 1990, there were 5300 million people. By the year 2000, the world's population is expected to be over 6 billion, and by 2050, 10 billion.

figure: number

In addition, most of these people will live in the poor areas of big cities. Now, 95 percent of the world's population lives in poorer countries. This means that most people on earth are poor. World population is growing fastest in cities. In 1950, only one Third World city had a population of 5 million. By the year 2000, there will be 46. So most of the world's people will live in cities.

Does the earth have enough natural **resources** to support this many people? Different scientists give different answers to this question. Some say that there are enough resources to
30 support more than 6 billion people. However, the richest countries, with a small percentage of the world's population, use most of the resources. If these resources could be **distributed** more equally around the world, there would be enough
35 for everyone.

Other scientists say that we must limit population growth because our resources are limited. Only 10 percent of the earth's land can be used for farming and another 20 percent for **raising**
40 animals. It is possible to increase the amount of farmland, but only a little. Some land in developing countries can be more productive if people start using modern farming **methods**, but this will not increase worldwide production very
45 much.

ways

We all know that there is a limited amount of petroleum. There are also limits to the amounts of iron (Fe), silver (Ag), gold (Au), and other **metals**. There is a limit to the water we can
50 use—most of the earth's water is salt water, and most of the fresh water is frozen at the North and South Poles.

Even some of the world's "natural" **disasters** are partly caused by overpopulation. We all
55 know about the terrible **famine**, with thousands of people dying of hunger, in Ethiopia in the 1980s. The famine area of Ethiopia used to be forested. Forests hold water in the ground, but in Ethiopia too many people cut down too many
60 trees for firewood. In only twenty years, the forests were gone. At the same time, there were several years without rain, and farmland became desert. There was no food, and people died of hunger.

terrible things that happen

It is difficult to say how many people the
65 earth can support, but it will help everyone if we can limit population growth before serious **shortages** develop. The problem is how to do it.

Each individual must decide to help limit population. Each person must decide how many
70 children to have. But there are many reasons that people want to have several children. Some people, because of their religion, believe that they must accept every child that God sends them. In countries where many children die before they
75 can grow up, people think they need to have several children. Then the parents will have someone to take care of them when they are old. In some countries, sons are more important to men than daughters. They and their wives keep
80 having children until they have several sons.

Research has repeatedly shown that the **average** Third World woman has more children than she wants. Among the women who do not think they have too many children, half of them
85 do not want any more. They think they already have enough. However, **although** millions of women in the world want to limit the size of their families, they cannot always find a safe way to have fewer children. Safe birth-**control** methods
90 for family planning are not **available** to everyone.

Governments and international organizations can **provide** safe, inexpensive birth-control methods. Individuals can decide to use them. Then the world population growth can **decrease**
95 instead of continuing to increase.

give

A Vocabulary

limit	figures	method	shortage
control	increases	raise	disaster
although	provide	overpopulated	resources

1. ________________ most journalists studied journalism in college, some older writers never attended a university.
2. Can you explain the ________________ for changing salt water to fresh water?
3. The number of injuries from automobile accidents ________________ every year.
4. Some countries are poor because they have very few natural ________________.
5. The Red Cross helps when there is a ________________.
6. These are all ________________: 1, 75, 293.
7. Some governments ________________ scholarships so people can attend a university.
8. A lack of rain can cause a water ________________.
9. China has more than a billion people. Is it ________________?
10. There is a ________________ of twenty minutes for this short test. Students must turn in their papers at the end of twenty minutes.

B Vocabulary

control	international	metals	average
decreasing	individual	distribution	famine
limit	raised	available	population

1. What is the ________________ of your country? Is it increasing?
2. ________________ are one kind of natural resources.
3. The population of Ireland is ________________. There are fewer people than there were 10 years ago.
4. The ________________ of 8, 5, 9, 3, and 6 is 6.2.
5. Some children behave badly and their parents can't ________________ them.
6. Coffee is ________________ in Central and South America.
7. When there is a ________________ in a country, other countries send food for ________________ to the hungry people.

8. Every person in the class is a different kind of
________________.
9. People build houses of the materials that are
________________ in the area.
10. The United Nations is an ________________ organization.

C Vocabulary Review

skill	tent	each other	blind
diary	frequently	surrounded	adventure
exhausted	civil war	yet	ashore

1. Mr. Rossi was ________________ after driving for 10 hours.
2. Our children had a wonderful ________________. They went camping in Canada, slept in a ________________, and helped cook their food outdoors over an open fire.
3. Typing is a very useful ________________ for students. They can learn by practicing.
4. The world is overpopulated, ________________ people keep having large families.
5. Alice injured her eyes in an accident. Now she is
________________.
6. There was a terrible ________________ in Spain in the 1930s. Almost a million people died.
7. Some composition teachers have the students keep a
________________. They write about their activities and their thoughts.
8. Mexican and African students have to speak English to
________________.
9. The children ________________ their teacher who was giving away free candy.
10. Glen ________________ goes to the movies on weekends.

World Population

Date	Population
10,000 B.C.	10,000,000
A.D.1	300,000,000
1750	625,000,000
1850	1,130,000,000
1950	2,510,000,000
1990	5,300,000,000
2000	6,600,000,000
2050	10,000,000,000

World's Largest Urban Areas

Tokyo/Yokohama, Japan	27,000,000
Mexico City, Mexico	20,207,000
São Paolo, Brazil	18,052,000
Seoul, South Korea	16,270,000
New York City, U.S.A.	14,625,000
Osaka/Kobe/Kyoto, Japan	13,826,000
Bombay, India	11,777,000
Calcutta, India	11,663,000
Buenos Aires, Argentina	11,518,000
Rio de Janeiro, Brazil	11,428,000
Moscow, Russia	10,367,000
Los Angeles, U.S.A.	10,060,000

The World's Largest Countries in Population

China	1,134,000,000
India	853,400,000
U.S.A.	250,000,000
Indonesia	179,100,000
Brazil	155,600,000
Russia	149,530,000
Japan	123,000,000
Nigeria	119,000,000
Bangladesh	113,340,000
Pakistan	105,400,000
Mexico	81,140,000
Germany	79,100,000
Vietnam	65,000,000
Italy	57,600,000
United Kingdom	57,250,000
France	56,180,000

D Multiple Choice

For the rest of the book, there are no asterisks (*) before any questions. You have to decide if the answer is in one of the sentences, or if you have to figure it out yourself. In this exercise, use the text and the charts to answer the questions.

1. There were more than ______ as many people in 1990 as in 1950.
   a. twice   b. three times   c. four times

2. Between 1990 and 2000, the population will ______.
   a. more than double
   b. be more than three times as large
   c. increase by more than a billion

3. About ______ percent of the earth's land can be used for raising food.
   a. 10   b. 20   c. 30

4. A ______ is sometimes a natural disaster.
   a. plane accident   b. forest fire   c. ship sinking

5. In the Third World, ______ women want more children.
   a. most b. some c. no
6. Safe birth-control methods are ______.
   a. usually expensive
   b. available for some women
   c. never used by religious people
7. ______ are almost the same size.
   a. China and the U.S.
   b. Britain and Italy
   c. Mexico and Germany
8. ______ has the urban area with the largest population.
   a. Brazil b. Nigeria c. Japan
9. In ______, the population of the whole world was about the same as the population of China today.
   a. 1750 b. 1850 c. 1950
10. ______ has almost the same population as Moscow and Los Angeles together.
   a. Mexico City b. Calcutta c. Seoul

E Comprehension Questions

Use the text and charts to answer these questions.

1. Do more people live in developed or developing countries?
2. Explain the problem of distribution of natural resources.
3. Can the amount of farmland be increased?
4. Why can't we use most of the earth's water?
5. Which European countries are among the world's largest?
6. How many people can the earth support?
7. Give two reasons that people have big families.
8. Do most Third World women want a lot of children?
9. What was one of the causes of the famine in Ethiopia?
10. Which urban area of the world has the largest population?
11. Do you think your country has too many people? Give a reason for your answer.

F Main Idea

What is the main idea of paragraph 2 (lines 6–17)? Write it in a sentence.

G Two-Word Verbs

Learn these two-word verbs and then fill in the blanks with the right words. Use the correct verb form.

cut down —for example, cut down a tree
figure out—find the answer
make up —think of a new story or idea
hang up —end a telephone conversation
clear up —clouds disappear and the sun comes out

1. It was rainy and cloudy this morning, but now it is starting to ________________.
2. The big old tree in our front yard is dead. We have to ________________ it ________________.
3. I can't ________________ the answer to this math problem.
4. When Tom finished talking to his friend on the phone, he said "Goodbye" and ________________.
5. Mr. Hasegawa ________________ funny stories to tell his children.

H Irregular Verbs

Memorize these verb forms. Then put the right form of a verb in each of the blanks.

Simple	**Past**	**Past Participle**
freeze	froze	frozen
forbid	forbade	forbidden
sink	sank	sunk
shoot	shot	shot

1. The law ________________ driving over 40 kilometers an hour on side streets in the city. You can drive 60 or 75 on main streets.
2. A small sailboat hit a rock, and within an hour it had ________________.

3. ________________ food is quick and easy to cook.
4. Bob went hunting and ________________ a bear.

I Word Forms: Adjectives

Adjectives describe nouns. They are usually before the noun. They are sometimes after the verb **be**.

These are **serious** questions.
These questions are **serious**.

Participles are often used as adjectives. The third form of the verb is the past participle; for example, talk, talked, **talked** and freeze, froze, **frozen**. The **-ing** form of the verb is the present participle; for example, **talking**.

The world is **overpopulated**.
Increasing population is a problem.

Write the correct word forms in the blanks.

Verb	Noun	Adjective	Adverb
1.	history	historical	historically
2.	shortage	short	
3.	disaster	disastrous	
4. distribute	distribution		
5. populate	population		
6. care	care	careful	carefully
		careless	carelessly
7. use	use	useful	usefully
		useless	uselessly
8.	individual	individual	individually
9.	nation	national	nationally

1. Anne likes to read ________________ novels.
2a. The secretary was ________________ of paper and had to order some.
2b. There was a ________________ of coffee because thousands of coffee trees in Brazil froze.
3. A famine is ________________ for a country.
4. The professor always ________________ the test papers as soon as the bell rings.

5. What is the ________________ of your country?
6. If you are ________________ when you write your composition, you will probably get a good grade. If you write ________________, you may fail.
7. A sled is ________________ if you live in Kuwait.
8. The kind of car a person buys is an ________________ decision. Each person must decide ________________.
9. Baseball is the ________________ sport in the United States.

J Articles

Put an article in each blank if one is necessary.

1. Is _____ world overpopulated?
2. How many people can _____ earth support?
3. These are _____ serious questions that _____ people must think about.
4. _____ different scientists give _____ different answers to these questions.
5. _____ richest countries, with _____ small percentage of _____ world's population, use _____ most of _____ resources.
6. It is possible to increase _____ amount of _____ farmland, but only _____ little.
7. We all know that there is _____ limited amount of _____ petroleum.
8. We all know about _____ terrible famine, with _____ thousands of people dying of _____ hunger, in _____ Ethiopia in _____ 1980s.

K Guided Writing

Write one of these two short compositions.

1. What is your country doing to help the world population problem? Describe what it is doing. If it isn't doing anything, what do you think it should do? Why?

2. Describe life in your city 10 years from now if twice as many people live there.

Changes in the Family

LESSON

Pre-reading Questions

1. **How many people are in your family?**
2. **Where do the people in your family live?**
3. **How is your life different from your grandparents' lives?**

Context Clues

1. Saudi Arabian **society** is very different from Japan's. People dress differently in the 2 countries. Religion is very important in Saudi Arabia, but it isn't in Japan. Holidays and homes are different. Most Japanese live in large cities. Most Saudis do not. The languages are different. The lives of women are different.
   a. the way people spend their time
   b. everything about the life in a country
   c. the life of each individual woman
2. The aborigines have been in Australia for 10,000 years. Their **ancestors** probably came from South Asia.
   a. people in the family a long time ago
   b. people in the family in the future
   c. great-grandparents
3. Elaine is an electrician. She **earns** twelve dollars an hour.
   a. works
   b. is paid for working
   c. pays
4. Al has a difficult problem to **solve** for his engineering class.
   a. write b. read c. find the answer to
5. The **couple** next door to us has two children.
   a. two people b. a husband and wife c. a few

2

Changes in the Family

Sociologists study **society** and how it is organized. They study what a society believes and how it is changing. They explain how people behave, but not how they ought to behave.

Almost every society is based on the family. Some societies have **nuclear** families. In the nuclear family, the parents and children live together in one house. Other societies have **extended** families. In this kind of family, there are grandparents, parents, children, uncles, and other **relatives** all living together. In some societies, there are **tribes**. A tribe is a group of extended families that have the same **ancestors**. In North and South America, the **members** of each Indian tribe speak the same language. Each tribe in Africa has its own language too. In Saudi Arabia and the other Gulf countries, the tribes all speak Arabic.

member = one of a group

Sometimes the power of the extended family or the tribe is based on the land that it owns.

Everybody in a family knows how to behave as a family member. Children learn how to act like grownups by watching the adults in their family. They learn how a father or mother should behave. Everyone knows what the correct behavior is, and relatives like to talk about this. "Is

Kumiko acting the way a mother should act?" "Does Abdullah behave in the right way for a husband?"

30 It is hard to look at research about the family with our minds instead of our feelings. Each person is part of a family and a society and knows what a family should be like. It is hard to realize that one kind of family can fit a society very well, 35 even if it is very different from the family in our society.

Throughout history there have been slow changes in the family and in family life, but today the family is changing quickly. This change causes 40 many problems for the society and the individual.

in all parts of

One of the major reasons for this fast change in the family is the change in how people **earn** their money. Today more and more people work in **factories** that make automobiles, furniture, 45 clothes, and thousands of other products. Fewer people work on farms or make products at home. People work in **industry** instead. This change is called industrialization. The ownership of land in an industrial society is not as important as it was 50 when people lived in villages.

factory

For decades young people have been leaving farms and small towns to go to cities and work in factories. They often find a wife or husband in the city instead of marrying someone from their vil- 55 lage. They start their own family away from their old home. These young people often have more money than the old people in their family.

In village life, young people went to the old people with their questions and problems. The 60 old people had lived a long time and had more knowledge. However, as young people moved to cities, got more education, and learned technol- ogy, they discovered that the old people in their family did not have all the answers to their ques- 65 tions about life. Their new lives in the city were

too different from village life. Also, in some countries, the government started making laws about things the tribe used to decide.

Life continued to change, and the children of 70 these young people discovered that their city parents didn't always have the answers either. Life was changing too fast.

Since the end of World War II, industrialization has been increasing very fast throughout the 75 world. This is causing family life to change faster too. Societies are losing their extended families. More **married couples** want their own homes where they can live with their children.

couple = wife and husband

The West has had nuclear families instead of 80 extended families at least since the Industrial **Revolution**. The Industrial Revolution started in England around 1760, when people changed from making things by hand to making them in factories.

85 Western families are changing too. When people get a good education and good jobs, they can improve their lives. They realize that if they have fewer children, they can give the ones they have a better life. Now more women work outside 90 the home, and they delay having children. The size of families gets smaller. In the United States, some of these small nuclear families move several times, each time earning more money and improving their lives. Some young couples don't see 95 their parents very often. They don't think it is necessary to invite their parents to live with them when the parents grow old. Many of the old parents don't want to live with their grown children either.

100 As Third World countries industrialize, they find they are having the same problems that Western families have. If a country modernizes and industrializes fast, the family changes fast. Many old people want life to continue as it was.

105 Young people want to move ahead and change. These different ideas can cause problems in the family.

We can learn about these changes in the family from sociologists and understand why 110 problems are developing. It is helpful for us to understand what is happening to our societies, but each individual family must try to **solve** its problems for itself.

A Vocabulary

couple	solve	earn	revolution
throughout	ancestors	industrial	industry
tribes	extended	nuclear	sociologists

1. The ______ family is larger than the ______ family.
2. There have been some civil wars between different African ______ living in the same country.
3. The ______ of everyone in Canada came from other countries. The Indians were the first to arrive.
4. How much money does a secretary ______?
5. Mr. and Mrs. Gorder are a married ______.
6. Japan is an ______ nation. It has heavy and light ______.

B Vocabulary

extend	industrial	learn	solve
member	factory	sociologist	throughout
revolution	societies	tribe	relatives

1. Maria is from Mexico, but she has several ______ in California. Three of her aunts live there with their families.
2. Sam works in an airplane ______.
3. Karl is a ______ of the International Students Organization.
4. A ______ does research about ______ throughout the world.
5. Governments ______ the world are trying to ______ the problems in their country.
6. The Russian ______ was in 1917. There was a complete change in government.

C Vocabulary Review

Match each word with its definition.

1. blizzard ____________
2. inland ____________
3. wool ____________
4. pony ____________
5. overeat ____________
6. inferior ____________
7. trade ____________
8. break down ____________
9. superior ____________
10. work out ____________

a. small horse
b. buying and selling
c. worse
d. stop running or working
e. a kind of cloth
f. a bad snow and wind storm
g. missionaries
h. exercise
i. anthropology
j. away from the ocean
k. eat more than you should
l. better than

D True/False/Not Enough Information

_______ 1. Sociologists tell us how people should behave so they can improve their society.
_______ 2. Members of a tribe all have the same ancestors.
_______ 3. Each individual learns how to fit into the family and society by copying the people around her or him.
_______ 4. The family is changing fast because of industrialization.
_______ 5. In many countries, the lives of young people are very different from the lives of their grandparents.
_______ 6. The West had extended families until the twentieth century.
_______ 7. When a country modernizes fast, the family changes fast.
_______ 8. The Industrial Revolution was a civil war in England. People fought about the ownership of land.
_______ 9. As countries industrialize, the family size decreases.

E Comprehension Questions

1. What is a nuclear family?
2. What is a tribe?
3. Why can't the old people in a family always help young people solve their problems?
4. When did industrialization start increasing throughout the world?

5. Why do many American families move several times?
6. Is your country already industrialized, or is it now developing industries?

F Main Idea

What is the main idea of paragraph 2 (lines 5–18)? Write it in a sentence.

G Word Forms: Adjectives

These are some common adjective suffixes: **-able, -al, -ful, -ive, -less, -like, -ous, -t, -y**.

Choose the right word form for each sentence.

	Verb	Noun	Adjective	Adverb
1.		society	social	socially
2.	industrialize	industry industrialization	industrial	
3.	earn	earnings		
4.		tribe	tribal	
5.	control	control	(un)controllable	(un)controllably
6.	limit	limit	limitless (un)limited	
7.		logic	(il)logical	(il)logically
8.		fame	famous	
9.		distance	distant	
10.	storm	storm	stormy	

1. Industrialization causes serious ________________ problems in a country.
2. Many Third World countries are trying hard to ________________.
3. Mr. and Mrs. Novak have to spend all of their ________________ to support their family.
4. There have been many ________________ wars in Africa.
5. A tire blew out and made the car ________________. It went out of ________________ and hit a tree.
6. Some people think there is a(n) ________________ amount of petroleum in the world, but someday we will run out.

7. Pat figured out the problem by using ________________.
8. Pele was a ________________ soccer player.
9. Alexandra David-Neel visited ________________, mysterious areas of the world.
10. ________________ weather caused serious problems for Vitus Bering.

H Prepositions

Put prepositions in the blanks.

1. Almost every society is based _____ the family.
2. _____ some societies, there are tribes.
3. _____ North America, the members _____ each Indian tribe speak the same language.
4. Sometimes the power _____ the family or the tribe is based _____ the land that it owns.
5. Children learn how to act _____ watching the adults _____ their family.
6. It is hard to look _____ research _____ the family _____ our minds instead _____ our feelings.
7. One _____ the major reasons _____ the fast change _____ the family is industrialization.
8. _____ decades young people have been leaving farms to go _____ cities and work _____ factories.
9. They start their own family _____ _____ their old home.
10. The Industrial Revolution was when people changed _____ making things _____ hand _____ making them _____ factories.

I Summarizing

A **summary** is all the important information in a paragraph. It is usually just one sentence. A summary of a complete reading text has a few sentences. Choose the summary sentence for these paragraphs.

1. Paragraph 1 (lines 1–4)
   a. Sociologists study how a society is changing.
   b. Sociologists study society.
   c. Sociologists study how people behave.

2. Paragraph 2 (lines 5–18)
    a. Societies have extended and nuclear families and sometimes tribes.
    b. A nuclear family is small, and an extended family is much larger.
    c. Almost every society is based on the family, either nuclear or extended.

3. Paragraph 4 (lines 21–29)
    a. Everyone learns how to behave as a parent.
    b. Everyone learns how to behave from other family members.
    c. Children learn how to behave by watching adult family members.

4. Paragraph 6 (lines 37–40)
    a. The family is changing fast today, and this causes problems.
    b. When families change, it causes problems for the individual.
    c. The family is changing faster today than before.

5. Paragraph 7 (lines 41–50)
    a. One cause of this change is working in factories.
    b. One cause of this change is owning land.
    c. One cause of this change is industrialization.

J Guided Writing

Write one of these two short compositions.

1. In your country, how are the family lives of you and your friends different from the family lives of your grandparents when they were young? Give examples.

2. Right now, do you live in a nuclear family or in an extended one? What do you think your family life will be like in the future? What kind of family will your children and grandchildren live in? Why do you think this?

Women and Change

LESSON

Pre-reading Questions

1. **In your country, do girls get the same education as boys? Why or why not?**
2. **Who does most of the work in your house?**
3. **How many women work in the government of your country? What do they do?**

Context Clues

1. Dean grew up on a farm, and he plans to study **agriculture**. Then he wants to buy a farm of his own.

   a. biology　　b. farming　　c. sociology

2. Dean's family has a small farm. They have two **fields** of wheat, one of corn, and several of vegetables. They use another **field** for their cows and horses.

   a. a garden

   b. the area of a farm where grass or other plants grow

   c. the place where farmers keep their animals

3. Mrs. Martin has a good job. She **trains** new workers for McDonald's. They have to learn how to do their jobs before they can start work.

   a. teaches　　b. travels　　c. raises

4. Tom has to **prepare** for his parents' visit to his apartment. He is going to clean and then buy food so he can cook dinner.

   a. telephone　　b. invite　　c. get ready

5. Amadou **is supposed to** give a report in class tomorrow. He didn't prepare, so he is not going to class.

   a. should　　b. might　　c. can

3

Women and Change

"Women hold up half the sky." This is an old Chinese saying. However, research shows that perhaps women do more than their **share** of "holding up the sky."

5 Many reports have been **published** on the conditions and **rights** of women throughout the world. Some of the news in the reports is very good. For example, 90 percent of all countries have **official** organizations to improve the lives 10 of women. More than half of the countries have laws to **protect** the rights of women, and 90 percent of all countries have passed laws to give women equal pay for equal work. WHO (World Health Organization) and UNICEF (United Na-15 tions Children's Fund) have programs to improve the health of people in Third World countries, especially women and children. More than half of the women in the world now have birth-control methods available. Almost half of the children in 20 school now are girls, a big change from the past, because in many countries education was not available to girls.

The reports also have bad news. Although most countries have official organizations to im-25 prove women's lives, many of these organizations don't do anything. Women make up 50 percent of the world's population, but in nearly 66 percent of all working hours, the work is done by women.

They do most of the **domestic** work, for example, cooking and washing clothes. Millions of women also work outside the home. Women hold almost 40 percent of all the world's jobs. For this work, they earn only about half as much as men, and of course they earn nothing for their domestic work.

Fewer than 10 percent of places in government are held by women. More than half of the people who can't read and write are women. These women who are still **illiterate** are the most **frightened** of trying to improve their lives. Being illiterate doesn't mean they are not intelligent. It does mean it is difficult for them to change their lives.

afraid

In developing countries, where ¾ of the world's population lives, women produce more than half of the food. In Africa 80 percent of all **agricultural** work is done by women. There are many programs to help poor countries develop their agriculture. However, for years these programs **provided** money and **training** for men but not for women. Now this is changing. International organizations and programs run by developed nations are helping women, **as well as** men, improve their agricultural production.

farming

provided = gave
training = teaching

In parts of Africa, this is a **typical** day for a village woman. At 4:45 a.m., she gets up, washes, and eats. It takes her a half hour to walk to the **fields**, and she works there until 3:00 p.m. She collects firewood and gets home at 4:00. She spends the next hour and a half **preparing** food to cook. Then she collects water for another hour. From 6:30 to 8:30, she cooks. After dinner, she spends an hour washing the dishes and her children. She goes to bed at 9:30 p.m.

usual

getting ready

In Pakistan women spend 60 hours a week on housework. In Italy around 80 percent of

mothers who work outside the home also do all of the housework. Their husbands don't usually help them.

70 Should there be a change in the lives of women? **Are** women **supposed to** do the housework? Should they work outside the home? Will an improvement happen in women's lives? Do they need improvement? Different people have 75 different answers to these questions.

should

The family is changing **rapidly** in many societies. Any change in the family **affects** women. Any change in the lives of women affects the family and the society. Governments have already 80 passed some laws affecting women. The changes now happening in the family and society will probably continue.

fast

A Vocabulary

provides	prepared	published	official
agriculture	illiterate	training	supposed to
affect	rights	protected	domestic

1. What book company ________________ this book?
2. Are you ________________ for the big test tomorrow?
3. A ________________ worker does a family's housework.
4. Hot and cold weather ________________ people in different ways.
5. Firefighters need ________________ before they can put out fires.
6. Caves ________________ some people from the weather thousands of years ago.
7. In some countries, schools must give ________________ exams at the end of the year. In others, each teacher writes an exam.
8. You are ________________ come to class on time.

B Vocabulary

share	frighten	illiterate	right
agriculture	training	protect	field
as well as	domestic	rapidly	typical

1. The children started fighting because one boy took more than his ________________ of the cake.
2. Some movies ________________ children so they can't sleep.
3. The world's population is increasing ________________.
4. Marge helped her friend finish her work. This was ________________ of Marge. She helps people a lot.
5. ________________ is another word for "farming."
6. Everyone has the ________________ to enough food, a place to live, medical care, and an education.
7. People who can't read and write are ________________.
8. There are some horses in the ________________ behind the farmhouse.

C Vocabulary Review

Match the words with their meaning.

1. relative ________________	a. a person who studies society
2. individual ________________	b. pass things out
3. population ________________	c. get larger
4. increase ________________	d. get smaller
5. sociologist ________________	e. number
6. method ________________	f. person
7. shortage ________________	g. number of people in an area
8. distribute ________________	h. way
9. disaster ________________	i. natural resources
10. decrease ________________	j. family member
11. figure ________________	k. frequent
	l. not enough
	m. a terrible happening

HOURS IN A WOMAN'S DAY IN DEVELOPING COUNTRIES

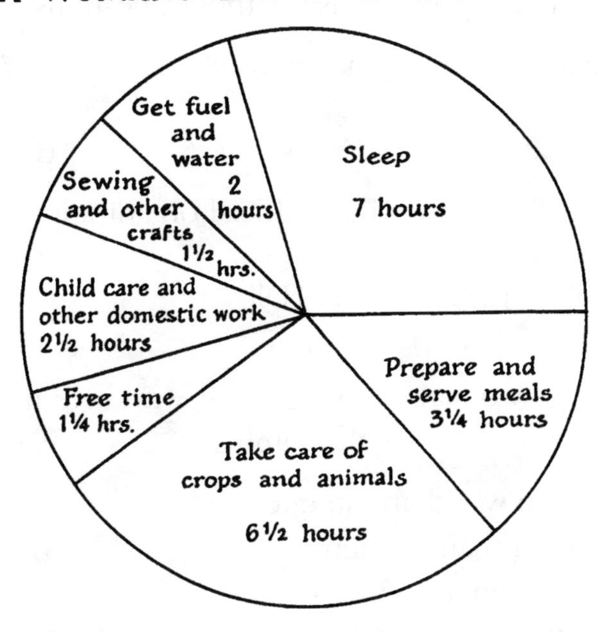

MEN'S AND WOMEN'S WORK IN AFRICA

	Percentage of Total Work in Hours	
	Men	**Women**
Cuts down forests, prepares fields	95	5
Turns the soil	70	30
Plants seeds and cuttings	50	50
Hoes and weeds	30	70
Gathers crops	40	60
Carries crops home	20	80
Stores crops	20	80
Processes food crops	10	90
Sells the extra crops	40	60
Carries water and fuel	10	90
Cares for domestic animals	50	50
Hunts	90	10
Feeds and cares for the family	5	95

SOURCE: UN Handbook on Women in Africa

D Multiple Choice

Use the text and the charts to answer these questions.

1. In Africa a village woman spends about ______ of her day farming.
   a. ¼ b. ⅓ c. ½
2. ______ of all countries have official organizations to improve the life of women.
   a. All but 90 percent b. Half c. All but 10 percent
3. The average woman earns ______ the average man.
   a. more than b. the same as c. less than
4. ______ in the world are literate.
   a. More men than women
   b. More women than men
   c. About the same number of women and men
5. In Africa, ______ of the farmwork is done by men.
   a. 80 percent b. 50 percent c. 20 percent
6. A typical African woman spends ______ collecting firewood daily.
   a. an hour b. 2 hours c. half an hour
7. An African village man does about half of the ______.
   a. weeding b. planting c. hunting
8. In Africa, village ______ carry most of the crops, water, and fuel.
   a. men b. women c. children

E Comprehension Questions

1. What does "women hold up half the sky" mean?
2. How many countries have laws to protect the rights of women?
3. Do you know any older women who are illiterate? If you do, why didn't they go to school?
4. Give a reason why some women work more hours than men.
5. Why do you think most Italian men don't help with the housework?

F Main Idea

What is the main idea of this reading text? Write one or two sentences.

G Scanning

Scan the reading text to find these answers. Write a short answer and the number of the line where you found the answer.

1. What percentage of jobs are held by women?
2. What percentage of government jobs are held by women?
3. What percentage of countries have laws about equal pay?
4. In Africa, what percentage of farmwork do women do?
5. How many hours a day do Pakistani women spend doing housework?
6. What percentage of women have birth-control methods available?
7. What percentage of children in school are boys?

H Articles

Put articles in the blanks if they are necessary.

1. This is ______ old Chinese saying.
2. Some of ______ news in ______ report is very good.
3. For example, 90 percent of all ______ countries now have ______ official organizations to improve ______ lives of ______ women.
4. Forty-one percent of ______ children in ______ school now are ______ girls.
5. ______ millions also work outside ______ home.
6. Sixty percent of ______ people who can't read are ______women.
7. In ______ Africa, 60 percent of all agricultural work is done by ______ women.
8. In ______ Africa, this is ______ typical day for ______ village woman.

I Word Forms

There is always a noun after an article. There might be an adjective before the noun.

> Women do most of the **housework**.
> An illiterate **person** cannot read or write.

	Verb	Noun	Adjective	Adverb
1.	publish	publication publisher		
2.	protect	protection	(un)protected protective	protectively
3.		(il)literacy	(il)literate	
4.	frighten	fright	frightening	frighteningly
5.		agriculture	agricultural	agriculturally
6.	provide	provision		
7.	train	training		
8.		type	typical	typically
9.	prepare	preparation		
10.	affect	effect	(in)effective	(in)effectively

1. *Newsweek* is a popular ________________.
2a. The police provide ________________ for the people in a country.
2b. Workers in dangerous jobs wear ________________ clothing.
3. ________________ is not a problem in Japan.
4. Ms. Baker had a ________________ experience last night. A strange man was in her house when she got home from work late.
5. Very few people work in ________________ in northern Russia. It is not an ________________ area.
6a. The teachers will ________________ food for the party.
6b. Explorers have to take a lot of ________________ with them.
7. You have to ________________ to be a police officer. ________________ is necessary.
8. What ________________ of student are you? Are you a ________________ college student? A good student ________________ studies a lot.
9. It is difficult to give a speech without ________________.
10. Exercise has a good ________________ on the muscles. If you exercise ________________, you will have strong muscles.

J Connecting Words

Use the word **but** to connect a sentence from the second column with one from the first column. Use a comma before **but**. Write the new sentences on a separate piece of paper.

1. Some of the news in the reports is good.
2. Half of the world's children are girls.
3. Many women work outside the home.
4. Rich countries have the fewest people.
5. It is possible to increase the amount of farmland.
6. There is enough water in the world.

a. Only 41 percent go to school.
b. They use the most natural resources.
c. It can be increased only a little.
d. Some of it is bad.
e. Most of it is salt water.
f. Their husbands don't help them with the housework.

K Guided Writing

Write one of these two short compositions.

1. Is it easy to change the life of women in a society? Give reasons for your answer.
2. In your country, is the life of a young woman today different from the lives of young women fifty years ago? Give examples.

Rain Forests

LESSON

Pre-reading Questions

1. **Do you have forests in your country? Describe them.**
2. **Compare the number of trees in your country with the number of trees there 100 years ago. Do you think there are more trees, fewer trees, or about the same number?**
3. **Name a living thing that could not live without the rain forest.**

Context Clues

1. The North Pole is in a cold **region** of the earth.
   a. temperature b. frozen c. area

2. Animals **such as** lions, hippopotamuses, and elephants live in Africa.
   a. for example b. however c. although

3. Babies are **tiny** when they are born.
   a. half grown b. very small c. ancient

4. Twenty-five is a **quarter** of 100.
   a. ¼ b. ⅓ c. ½

5. We get beef and milk from **cattle**.
   a. cows b. sheep c. goats

6. Miss Li **no longer** lives in Hong Kong. She moved to Taiwan.
   a. shorter b. plans to c. not any more

4

Rain Forests

Tropical rain forests are found in the Amazon **region** of South America, Central America, Africa, and South and Southeast Asia. They are very old, thick forests where it rains more than 1.8 meters per year. The oldest rain forest in the world is in Sarawak. It is 10 million years old. In rain forests, huge trees 45 meters high have their first **branches** about 10 meters above the ground. Below the trees, there is another **level** of plants—many kinds of smaller trees, **bushes**, and flowers. The Sarawak forest has 2500 different kinds of trees.

area

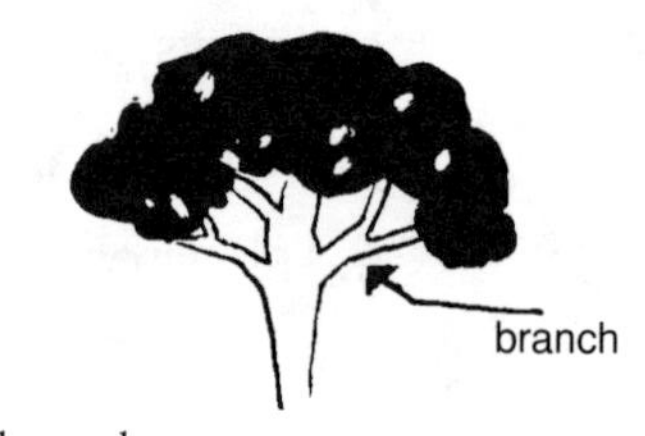

branches

Each level of the rain forest is its own world. The lower level is protected by the trees above. The temperature and **humidity** (the amount of water or **moisture** in the air) stay about the same in the lower level. There is not much sunlight. In the upper level, the sun, rain, and wind change the temperature and humidity often.

An amazing animal world lives in the upper level. There are monkeys, members of the cat family, birds, and **insects such as bees**, **butterflies**, and many kinds of **flies**. Other animals that usually live on the ground also live here—mice, **ants**, and even **earthworms**.

such as = for example

bee, butterfly, ant, fly earthworm

This upper level of the forest is thick with plant life because the trees are covered with other plants. Most plants get **nutrients** from the ground through their **roots**. These plants in the upper level take their nutrients from the trees they live on and from the other plants that die there.

food

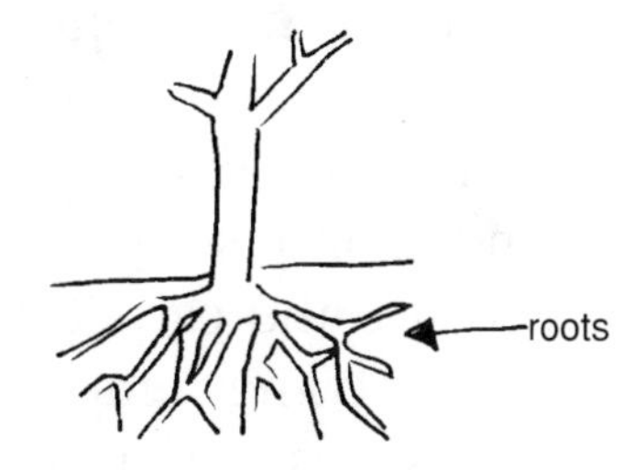

The animals need "streets" so they can move along the upper level without going down to the ground. They make **paths** along the branches of the trees. A researcher found a path that **stretched** for 18 meters in one tree. One kind of **tiny** ant makes a path only 3 millimeters wide.

very small

Now **humans** are **destroying** the earth's tropical rain forests. About 80,000 square kilometers are being destroyed every year. About 1/4 of the **destruction** comes from people cutting down trees for fuel. Another **quarter** is destroyed when people cut down trees to make grassland for their **cattle**.

people

noun for *destroy*

1/4

cattle

People cut down the rest of the trees so they can sell the wood or start farms. Cities all over the world are growing and want huge buildings. For example, the Japanese used 5000 trees from the Sarawak rain forest to build one tall building. If people continue to cut that many trees in the Sarawak forest, all the trees will be gone in 8 years.

The world needs more food, and it seems like a good idea to clear the rain forests and use the land for agriculture. Land that can support these huge, thick forests must be very rich in nutrients. But it isn't. This is another surprising thing about rain forests.

Most of the land in tropical rain forests is very poor. The plants are able to live because of all the dead leaves and other plant parts that fall to the ground. This carpet of dead plants provides nutrients for the living plants.

65 When the land is cleared for agriculture, there are **no longer** any plants left to die and provide nutrients for living plants. The **cycle** is broken. Agriculture is unsuccessful because the land cannot support it. Trees cannot grow again 70 because the carpet of dead plants is gone. The land becomes empty and useless.

not any more

circle, something that happens again and again

Is this important? What does it matter to a Japanese businessperson, a French farmer, or an Arab student that people are destroying rain for- 75 ests thousands of kilometers away?

Do you ever take medicine? Do you wear running shoes? Do you use envelopes when you mail letters? Rain forests make these things possible.

Rain forests cover less than 6 percent of the 80 earth's area, but they have 100,000 kinds of plants, probably half of all the kinds of plants on the earth. Three-fourths of all known kinds of plants and animals call the rain forest their home. Twenty percent of our different kinds of medicine 85 comes from rain forests. The **glue** on an envelope and in shoes comes from tropical plants. Rain forests provide materials for hundreds of other products.

Rain forests are also very important to the 90 world's climate. The Amazon rain forest alone receives about 30 to 40 percent of the total rainfall on the earth and produces about the same percentage of the world's **oxygen** (O). Some scientists believe that the decreasing size of rain 95 forests will affect the climate on the earth, making it uncomfortable or even dangerous for life.

Saving our rain forests is an international problem. One country, or even a few countries, cannot solve the problem alone. The nations of 100 the world must work together to find a **solution** before it is too late.

noun for *solve*

A Vocabulary

bush	path	branch	such as
humans	quarter	no longer	solution
insects	tiny	level	roots
destruction	cattle	tropical	humidity

1. Flies, ants, and bees are examples of ________________.
2. An insect is a ________________ animal.
3. When students do well in their English classes, they move up to the next ________________.
4. Masako had to leave the university and go home. She is ________________ studying English.
5. The lives of most ________________ are changing fast.
6. Anne and Ken like to walk on a ________________ along the river in the evening.
7. A ________________ is part of a tree.
8. A ________________ is a low plant.
9. ________________ are cows.
10. Malayasia is a ________________ country. The temperature and the ________________ are both high there.
11. We must find a ________________ to the problem of overpopulation.
12. The ________________ of most plants are below the ground.

B Vocabulary

fly	cycle	nutrients	path
ant	bee	moisture	region
oxygen (O)	such as	butterfly	earthworms
stretch	glue	quarter	no longer

1. The ________________, ________________, ________________, and ________________ are all insects.
2. A ________________ is a circle.
3. Humans need to eat the right food in order to get the right ________________.
4. Most of North Africa is a desert ________________.
5. Carol needs some ________________ to fix a broken plate.

6. People in Latin American countries _______________ Ecuador, Peru, and Venezuela speak Spanish.
7. The Andes Mountains _______________ from Colombia to Chile.
8. A _______________ is ¼.
9. Most _______________ live under the ground.
10. The amount of _______________ in the air is called humidity.
11. _______________ is necessary for life.

C Vocabulary Review

rubber	ivory	treat	colony
attitude	although	average	metal
famine	industry	revolution	extended
nuclear	tribes	frightened	field

1. There are two kinds of families, _______________ and _______________.
2. The Indian _______________ in the Americas came from Siberia.
3. Mr. Green has an excellent _______________ about visiting a foreign country. He wants to learn everything about it that he can.
4. You don't have to like everybody, but you should _______________ everyone the right way.
5. _______________ Joe doesn't like to fly, he is going to Hawaii on his vacation.
6. Tires are made from _______________.
7. Some _______________ comes from elephants, but it is illegal to bring it into many countries now.
8. The United States was a British _______________ until 1776. Then the American _______________ made it a separate country.

D True/False/Not Enough Information

_______ 1. Some rain forests are not in the tropics.
_______ 2. There is more change in weather in the upper level of a rain forest than in the lower.
_______ 3. In the upper level, some plants support the life of the other plants.
_______ 4. Plants get nutrients through their branches.
_______ 5. People destroy about 20,000 square kilometers of tropical rain forest every year so they can burn the wood.
_______ 6. The land in tropical rain forests is rich.
_______ 7. Tropical rain forest land can support forests although it cannot support agriculture.
_______ 8. Material from rain forests is used to make cassette tapes.
_______ 9. Earthworms make paths on the branches of trees in rain forests.
_______ 10. There are rain forests in Brazil.
_______ 11. Rain forests have 100,000 kinds of plants.

E Comprehension Questions

1. How is the weather in the lower level of a rain forest different from the weather in the upper level?
2. Why is it amazing to find mice and earthworms in the upper level?
3. Where do most plants in the upper level get their nutrients?
4. Why do people cut down trees in rain forests?
5. Where do plants in the lower level get their nutrients?
6. What happens to the land when the trees are cut down?
7. Why are rain forests important to the world's climate?
8. What are some other reasons they are important to all of us?

F Paraphrasing

Use your own words to say the same ideas as these sentences from the text. It is not necessary to use the same number of sentences. You may use more.

1. The plants in the upper level take their nutrients from the trees they live on and from the other plants that die there.
2. When the land is cleared for agriculture, there are no longer any plants left to die and provide nutrients for living plants.

G Main Idea

1. Which sentence is the main idea of paragraph 3 (lines 20–25)?
2. Write your own sentence for the main idea of paragraph 13 (lines 79–88).

H Cause and Effect

Match the causes in the second column with the effects in the first column. Write the letter of the effect by the number of the cause.

Cause	Effect
1. The upper level is thick with plants.	a. The weather doesn't change much in the lower level.
2. The trees are all cut down.	b. They make paths along branches.
3. A carpet of dead plants provides nutrients.	c. The land cannot support agriculture.
4. Animals want to travel in the upper level.	d. Tropical plants can live on poor land.
5. The lower level is protected by the upper level.	e. Tropical land becomes useless.

I Word Forms

	Verb	Noun	Adjective	Adverb
1.		tropics	tropical	
2.		humidity	humid	
3.		moisture	moist	
4.		human humanity	(in)human	(in)humanly
5.	destroy	destruction	destructive	destructively
6.	solve	solution		
7.	endanger	danger	dangerous endangered	dangerously
8.		(in)ability (dis)ability	(un)able	ably
9.	(dis)appear	(dis)appearance		
10.	own	owner ownership		

1. Indonesia is in the ________________.
2. It's hot and ________________ today.
3. It's humid today and my skin is ________________.

4a. ________________ beings must work together to solve the world's problems.

4b. Some prisoners want to escape because the jailers treat them ________________.

5. War is ________________. It takes human life and ________________ cities, villages, and agricultural land.
6. Dan finally figured out the ________________ to his math problem.
7. The tropical rain forests of the world are ________________. They are in ________________ of being destroyed.

8a. Does the United Nations have the ________________ to improve the lives of women?

8b. Deafness and blindness are examples of a physical ________________.

8c. The ________________ to speak English is a problem for an international businessperson.

9. The ________________ of 80,000 square kilometers of rain forest a year is a serious problem.
10. Who is the ________________ of that beautiful Mercedes Benz?

J Noun Substitutes

Find each word and decide what it is a substitute for. It is usually a substitute for one word, but it might be for a whole sentence.

> In parts of Africa, this is a typical day for a village woman. At 4:45 a.m., **she** gets up, washes, and eats.
>
> **She** is a substitute for **a village woman**.

1. page 94, line 3 **they**
2. page 95 line 30 **their**
3. line 31 **they**
4. line 32 **there**
5. line 33 **they**
6. line 58 **it**
7. line 58 **this**
8. page 96 line 69 **it**
9. line 72 **this**
10. line 80 **they**

K Articles

Put an article in each blank if it is necessary.

1. Below ______ trees there is another level of plants.
2. Each level of ______ forest is its own world.
3. ______ temperature and humidity (______ amount of ______water or______ moisture in ______ air) stay about ______ same.
4. In ______ upper level, ______ sun, ______ rain, and ______ wind change ______ temperature and ______ humidity often.
5. Most plants get ______ nutrients from ______ ground through their roots.
6. These plants in ______ upper level take their nutrients from ______ trees they live on and from ______ other plants that die there.
7. ______ researcher found ______ path that stretched for ______ 18 meters in one tree.
8. One kind of ______ tiny ant makes ______ path only 3 millimeters wide.

L Guided Writing

Write one of these two short compositions.

1. Why are rain forests important?
2. You are walking through a rain forest. Describe what you see, hear, smell, and touch.

The Garbage Project

LESSON

Pre-reading Questions

1. What are the people in the picture doing?
2. Where do people in your country put garbage?
3. Can garbage be dangerous? Why?

Context Clues

1. Tom has books, pencils, a radio, a cup, some cassettes, and several other **objects** on his desk.

   a. books b. things c. writing materials

2. There are plants that contain **poison** in both deserts and rain forests. If you eat one, you will get sick or even die.

   a. a kind of medicine
   b. a plant that can live on poor land
   c. something that can kill you

3. When the teacher gave fifteen pages of homework, the students **protested**.

   a. said they didn't like it
   b. asked what the page numbers were
   c. asked for more

4. Don't dress up for the party tonight. Just wear your **ordinary** clothes.

   a. best b. oldest c. usual

5

The Garbage Project

Dr. William Rathje teaches **archaeology** at the University of Arizona in Tucson, Arizona, and directs the **Garbage** Project. One of the authors, N.N., asked Dr. Rathje (W.R.) about this project.

archaeology: scientific study of old things

5 N.N.: What is garbage?

W.R.: Garbage now is anything you throw away, the same as **waste**.

garbage

N.N.: What is the Garbage Project?

W.R.: Archaeologists study broken **objects** and animal bones, old garbage, to learn important things about ancient societies. We look at fresh garbage to learn important things about modern society. The Garbage Project started twenty years ago. Groups of students study garbage in many places, including Tucson, Miami, New York, San Francisco, Chicago, Toronto, and Mexico City.

objects: things

N.N.: What do you study about garbage?

W.R.: One thing we study is **landfills**, the places where cities put garbage. Landfills are growing. Scientists say 67 percent of garbage in landfills should disappear naturally and quickly. But the Garbage Project proved that garbage disappears very slowly in landfills. Even in cities where it rains a lot, we found newspapers from

1948, forty-year-old hot dogs, and lettuce from 1970. Garbage just stays there.

N.N.: Is that because the garbage is in plastic bags?

30 W.R.: No. The bags always break open, but there still isn't enough air and moisture moving through the garbage to make it disappear.

N.N.: Sometimes **explosions** in landfills kill people. Is your work **hazardous**?

explosion
dangerous

35 W.R.: Our work could be dangerous, but we wear special clothes and safety equipment. Students are very careful when they open bags of garbage.

N.N.: How should we **dispose of** garbage?

throw away

40 W.R.: The best way to dispose of garbage **depends on** what kind of garbage it is: regular garbage, hazardous waste, or **recyclables**, such as newspapers, glass bottles, and some metals. Regular garbage goes to regular landfills.

45 N.N.: Aren't landfills becoming full?

W.R.: Society makes millions of tons of garbage a day. Landfills close when they are full. There aren't many new ones because nobody wants to live near a landfill with the trucks, the wind, and 50 the smells. It's a **complicated** problem.

not simple, not easy

N.N.: Yes, people sometimes have **nonviolent** protests against new landfills. No one is hurt or gets into fights, but the protesters take **direct** action. They walk to the new landfills with signs. 55 They also take indirect action by writing letters to the government.

peaceful

So how do you dispose of hazardous waste?

W.R.: Hazardous waste contains **poisonous chemicals** or metals. We must keep it out of
60 regular landfills.

poison

N.N.: Do we have hazardous waste at home?

W.R.: **Ordinary** houses are full of hazardous waste. The most important hazardous waste in homes is **batteries**. When you throw them away
65 with your other garbage, they break open at the landfill. The poison inside them moves through rainwater and other liquids to the bottom of the landfill. Then it can **pollute** the natural water in the ground. We should use **rechargeable** batteries.
70 Another hazardous waste from homes is motor oil. Don't throw old motor oil on the ground or throw it in the garbage. It poisons the **environment**. We should recycle motor oil.
Paint is another kind of hazardous waste in
75 homes. Some cities have a "Paint Exchange Day." If you bring in open, unused blue paint and want red, they give you red. Sometimes they mix the paints together into strange colors. If you paint walls with them, you help save the environment.

usual, not different

batteries

make dirty

80 N.N.: Why don't all cities have recycling programs?

W.R.: Recycling garbage is expensive. It takes time, equipment, and special treatment. Toronto began the first recycling program in North Amer-
85 ica in 1982 with newspapers. Then it added glass and cans. The Garbage Project proved that, since 1982, Toronto has made the total amount of garbage going to its landfills 25 percent smaller by recycling.

90 N.N.: Should we **reuse** things?

use again

W.R.: Of course. Many societies have workers who go through the garbage for usable things. They protect the environment and save natural

resources. However, richer, more modern societ-
95 ies don't like people going near garbage. Often, going through garbage is against the law.

N.N.: What other things can the Garbage Project teach us?

W.R.: Societies begin small. They recycle and
100 reuse. Then, when they can grow more food or do more business or make better war, they become rich. They throw things away. Then the societies run out of resources, and they have to recycle and reuse things again. Now we're like the
105 second, richer societies. We must become like the first and third, recycling and reusing. We'll be here a lot longer if we can do that.

A health official said, "We're in deep trouble here. We have too much garbage, our landfills are
110 closing, and we can't open new ones because people don't want them. If we don't do something about our garbage, we're going to be buried in it." He said that in 1889.

A Vocabulary

poisonous	nonviolent	depends on	explosion
disposal	chemicals	hazard	objects
waste	forms	landfill	direct

1. We found some unusual ________________ on the beach.
2. The hole in the street is a ________________ to cars.
3. The meeting was peaceful, and no one was hurt or got into a fight because the people were ________________.
4. The noise from the terrible ________________ woke everyone up in the middle of the night.
5. Chemists have made thousands of new ________________.
6. Some chemicals are ________________.
7. Bottles, paper, and cans are examples of dry ________________.
8. After you cut the grass, please put it into a bag and take it to the ________________.

9. Some organizations try to change the laws of the country. Others go to the places where the problem exists to take ________________ action.
10. How healthy you are ________________ how well you take care of your body.
11. The ________________ of old automobiles is sometimes difficult.

B Vocabulary

rechargeable	ordinary	environment	protest
archaeologist	complicated	batteries	reuse
recycled	pollution	garbage	wastes

1. Don't throw that juice bottle away because it is empty. We can fill it with water and ________________ it.
2. Air ________________ is a serious problem in Mexico City.
3. Factories pollute the ________________.
4. ________________ people in many countries ________________ because their governments want to build landfills near their houses.
5. The paper in your newspaper is ________________. It was made out of old newspapers.
6. The problem was so ________________ that the engineer couldn't solve it.
7. The ________________ for my new camera are ________________. I just plug them in overnight, and in the morning, they are as good as new.
8. That ________________ smells terrible.
9. That woman is a famous ________________. She discovered an ancient city.

C Vocabulary Review: Antonyms

Match the words that mean the opposite.

1. warlike ____________	a. literate
2. be supposed to ____________	b. slowly
3. typical ____________	c. increase
4. illiterate ____________	d. underpopulated
5. individual ____________	e. peaceful
6. no longer ____________	f. unusual
7. rapidly ____________	g. rights
8. huge ____________	h. shouldn't
9. humid ____________	i. training
10. decrease ____________	j. group
11. overpopulated ____________	k. tiny
	l. still
	m. dry

D Multiple Choice

1. 1. The environment is ______.
   a. natural b. made by people c. both a and b

2. Poisonous chemicals pollute ______.
   a. water b. wastes c. explosions

3. The Garbage Project is about ______ years old.
   a. twenty b. ten c. fifty

4. The first recycling program in North America was in ______.
   a. the United States b. Mexico c. Canada

5. Garbage in landfills disappears ______.
   a. slowly b. completely c. quickly

6. The most serious hazardous waste in homes is ______.
   a. paint
   b. batteries
   c. motor oil

7. Dr. Rathje believes that ______.
   a. our society must make less garbage
   b. direct action is the only way to stop the building of new landfills
   c. people cannot change their behavior toward garbage

8. People protest against new landfills because ______.
   a. they do not like garbage
   b. they like to fight other people
   c. they do not want to live near landfills

9. Hazardous waste comes from ______.
   a. ordinary houses
   b. factories
   c. both a and b

Materials in Landfills

Paper Products (50%)
Other (20%)
Yard Waste & Food (13%)
Plastic (10%)
Metal (6%)
Glass (1%)

E Comprehension Questions

Use the text and chart to answer these questions.

1. Name three kinds of hazardous waste in homes.
2. Why is hazardous waste dangerous?
3. Why are we filling our landfills so fast?
4. What is the largest single kind of garbage in landfills?
5. What percentage of the garbage in a landfill is plastic?
6. What is the connection between the Garbage Project and archaeology?
7. Why did the Garbage Project go to Toronto?
8. What are three things that we can recycle?
9. Why do protesters take direct action against new landfills?

10. How can protesters take indirect action?
11. Do you think the problem of disposing of garbage is serious? Give a reason for your answer.

F Main Idea

1. Write a sentence that gives the main idea for the paragraph that starts on line 19.
2. Which sentence is the main idea of the last paragraph?

G Two-Word Verbs

check in —tell the airline that you are there for the flight or tell the hotel you are there for your room
drop out —stop going to school
get through—finish
put back —put something where it was before or where it belongs
think over —think about carefully

1. I can't give you my answer right away. I have to ________________ it ________________. I'll tell you next week.
2. You have to ________________ at the airport 45 minutes before your flight leaves.
3. Did you ________________ with your homework yet?
4. David didn't finish college. He ________________ after his second year.
5. Please ________________ the food ________________ in the refrigerator. Don't leave it out on the table.

H Compound Words

Use a word from the first column and one from the second column to make a compound word.

1. down a. work ______________________
2. far b. land ______________________
3. fire c. land ______________________
4. rain d. hill ______________________
5. half e. fall ______________________
6. sun f. ground ______________________
7. house g. off ______________________
8. grass h. light ______________________
9. under i. wood ______________________
10. farm j. way ______________________

I Connecting Words

Use **and** to connect a sentence from the first column with a sentence from the second column. Use a comma before **and**. Write your answers on a separate piece of paper.

1. Studying old garbage can teach us about ancient societies.
2. Students in the Garbage Project wear safety equipment.
3. We dispose of regular garbage in regular landfills.
4. Landfills close when they are full.
5. Hazardous waste contains poisonous chemicals.
6. The poison inside batteries can go to the bottom of a regular landfill.
7. Many societies have workers who go through the garbage for usable things.

a. They open bags of garbage very carefully.
b. They protect the environment.
c. Studying fresh garbage can teach us about modern society.
d. There aren't many new ones.
e. It can pollute the natural water in the ground.
f. We should dispose of hazardous waste in special landfills or by recycling.
g. We must keep it out of regular landfills.

J Summarizing

Which sentence is the summary of the paragraph that begins on these lines?

1. Line 46
   a. Having enough landfills is a complicated problem.
   b. Society makes a lot of garbage.
   c. Landfills smell bad.
2. Line 51
   a. Protesters take nonviolent direct action.
   b. Protesters can take action both directly and indirectly.
   c. Protesters try to stop the building of new landfills by carrying signs.
3. Line 99
   a. Societies begin small.
   b. Archaeologists study objects from ancient societies.
   c. Society today must recycle and reuse.

K Guided Writing

Write one of these two short compositions.

1. Describe the Garbage Project. Tell what it is, who is in it, what they do, and why.
2. What kind of hazardous waste do we have in our homes, and how can we dispose of it?

Unit 3

A Mishmash (A Hodgepodge)

The world is so full of a number of things,
I'm sure we should all be as happy as kings.

—Robert Louis Stevenson

The Roadrunner

LESSON

Pre-reading Questions

1. **Is this bird moving fast or slowly?**
2. **Does the bird eat only plants and bugs?**
3. **Have you ever seen a bird that looks like this in real life? Or maybe on television? (Hint: Beep Beep!)**

Context Clues

Circle the letter of the best meaning of the **bold** word.

1. Stop talking **immediately**. This is a test.
   a. in a few minutes b. right now c. soon

2. Bob received a videotape recorder as a **gift** from his parents on his birthday.
   a. present b. money c. package

3. This textbook has a **variety** of exercises.
   a. vocabulary b. few c. several different kinds

4. We will have the class picnic **even though** the weather isn't very nice.
   a. The weather isn't nice, so we won't have the picnic.
   b. The weather isn't nice, but we'll have the picnic anyway.
   c. We won't have the picnic because the weather isn't nice.

1

The Roadrunner

Beep Beep! People all over the world laugh at roadrunner cartoons, but the real bird is almost as funny as the cartoon.

The roadrunner lives in the desert region of 5 the southwestern United States and northern Mexico. It is a bird, but it can only fly about as much as a chicken can. People gave it its name because they usually see it running across a road, but, of course, it spends more time among the 10 plants in the desert than it does on roads.

The roadrunner is quite a large bird—about 45 centimeters long and 25 high. People laugh when it runs because it looks so funny. It holds its head straight out in front and its tail **sticks** 15 straight **out** in back. It takes long steps and can run 30 kilometers an hour.

It eats an amazing **variety** of food. Although it eats plants **once in a while**, it is mostly a meat eater. Most of its **diet** is insects, but it also catches 20 birds, mice, and other small animals. It is even brave enough to catch tarantulas, **snakes**, and black widow **spiders**.

variety: different kinds
once in a while: sometimes

In the spring, a **male** roadrunner begins looking for a **female** as a **mate**. When he finds 25 one, he gives her presents—a snake to eat or a **twig** (a tiny branch of a tree) to use in building a

snake
spider

nest. Then they build their nest, the female lays eggs, and they raise their young.

nest

Roadrunners can also become friendly with 30 people. One couple in Arizona feeds a pair of roadrunners that come one at a time every day and make a noise outside the window. If someone doesn't give the bird a piece of hamburger **immediately**, the bird **knocks** on the window 35 with its **beak**. Roadrunners are not **shy**.

right now

beak

In early spring, the bird doesn't eat the meat itself. It carries the meat to its nest to feed its young. Later on it brings the young bird to the house to beg for food itself.

40 When the woman **whistles**, the bird comes running. When the man walks out the **driveway**, the roadrunner walks along behind, like a dog or cat.

Another couple feeds a pair of roadrunners 45 that go right into the house. They will stand on a chair or table and watch television, and they seem really interested in what is happening on the **program**. In the spring, the male sometimes brings **gifts** to the couple—a leaf or twig for 50 building a nest, or an insect.

presents

In the winter, when nighttime temperatures in the desert can be 20° C colder than during the day, the weather doesn't become warm until the middle of the morning. The roadrunner has an 55 unusual way of keeping warm in this cold weather. In the early morning, the roadrunner stands with its back to the sun. It holds out its **wings** and lifts the **feathers** on its upper back. There is a dark **spot** on the skin under these 60 feathers. This spot collects heat from the sun and warms the bird's body. The bird doesn't need to use a lot of **energy** to keep warm the way that most birds do.

wing

feather

Some people in Mexican villages use road-65 runner meat as medicine. They believe that because

roadrunners can eat poisonous animals and not die, their meat should be good for human sickness.

Maybe we shouldn't laugh at the roadrunner. 70 **Even though** it looks funny when it runs, it has developed a special way to keep warm, and it can eat poisonous animals. It can even make friends with humans. It fits into its environment very well, and it isn't important that it looks funny.

although

A Vocabulary

variety	diet	male	female
mate	knock	driveway	feathers
even though	snakes	immediately	whistled
gift	special	stick out	couple

1. Some ________________ are dangerous, but most are not.
2. A ________________ connects the garage and the street.
3. There is a large ________________ of food in a supermarket.
4. A woman is a ________________, and a man is a ________________.
5. The class is going to the museum ________________ it is raining a little, and we have to walk.
6. The ________________ in China is based on rice and vegetables.
7. Birds have ________________.
8. Bill ________________ for a taxi, and one stopped.
9. Animals look for a ________________ in spring.
10. If you hear the fire alarm, leave the building ________________.
11. Joan received a car from her parents as a ________________ when she finished college.

B Vocabulary

knock	programs	spot	once in a while
spider	wing	stick out	energy
diet	hazardous	feather	immediately
shy	snake	nest	variety

1. An airplane has a ________________ on each side so it can fly.
2. When I heard a ________________ at the door, I went to answer it.
3. Mary watches television a lot, but she only goes to the movies ________________.
4. An insect has six legs; a ________________ has eight.
5. Don't ________________ your tongue; it is very impolite.
6. Jean has a ________________ on her new white jeans, and she can't get it out.
7. What television ________________ do you like to watch?
8. We burn wood, gas, coal, and oil for ________________.
9. Birds build a ________________ in the spring.
10. The little girl was hiding behind her father's legs because she was ________________.

C Vocabulary Review

Match the words with their definitions.

1. prepare ________________
2. literate________________
3. bush________________
4. cattle________________
5. publish________________
6. region________________
7. nonviolent________________
8. cycle________________
9. be supposed to________________
10. such as________________
11. quarter________________
12. object ________________

a. print and distribute books
b. should
c. one-fourth
d. get ready
e. for example
f. low plant
g. can read and write
h. area
i. tropical
j. cows
k. domestic
l. peaceful
m. circle
n. thing

D True/False/Not Enough Information

_______ 1. The roadrunner runs around the desert looking for food.
_______ 2. Roadrunners live only in Mexico and the United States.
_______ 3. The female gives the male gifts in the spring.
_______ 4. A roadrunner is afraid of people and stays away from them.
_______ 5. This bird can learn to depend on people.
_______ 6. A big difference between daytime and nighttime temperatures is typical in the desert.
_______ 7. A roadrunner uses a lot of energy keeping warm in winter.
_______ 8. The roadrunner is a typical bird.

E Comprehension Questions

1. Explain why the roadrunner is not a typical bird.
2. What does a roadrunner eat?
3. Why does a male give gifts to the female?
4. Why do people laugh at the roadrunner?
5. Explain how the roadrunner gets warm in winter.
6. Do you think sick people will get better if they eat roadrunner meat? Explain your answer.
7. Do you think it is a good idea to feed wild animals? Give a reason.
8. Explain how a roadrunner fits into its environment.

F Main Idea

Many paragraphs have a sentence that gives the main idea. It can be in different places in a paragraph.

1. Which sentence is the main idea of paragraph 4 (lines 17–22)?
2. Paragraph 10 (lines 51–63)?
3. Paragraph 11 (lines 64–68)?
4. Paragraph 12 (lines 69–74)?

G Word Forms

Nouns are often used to describe other nouns. The meaning is different than when the adjective form of the same word is used.

> Cuba had a **literacy** program in the 1960s.
> A **literate** person can read and write.

In which sentences in this exercise does a noun describe another noun? Choose the right word form for each sentence.

	Verb	Noun	Adjective	Adverb
1.		environment	environmental	environmentally
2.	complicate	complication	(un)compli-cated	
3.	pollute	pollution	(un)polluted	
4.	waste	waste	wasteful	wastefully
5.	explode	explosion explosive	explosive	explosively
6.	depend (on)	(in)dependence	(in)dependent	(in)dependently
7.		(non)violence	(non)violent	(non)violently
8.	vary	variety variation	various	
9.	specialize	specialty specialist	special	especially
10.	know	knowledge	(un)known knowledgeable	(un)knowingly knowledgeably

1. Water pollution is an ________________ problem.
2a. A disease can cause ________________ that make the person even sicker.
2b. This is a ________________ problem, and I can't find the solution.
3. Are there any ________________ rivers left in the world?
4. Some ________________ products from factories can be reused.
5. Some waste ________________ in a landfill. The waste was made of ________________.
6. Ghandi led India's ________________ movement.
7. There has been a lot of ________________ in Northern Ireland for several years.

8a. The amount of rainfall in the Australian desert ________________. In some years, there is only a little, and in other years, there is a lot.

8b. A supermarket sells a large ________________ of products.

8c. The "true/false/not enough information" exercises are a ________________ on the "true/false exercises."

9a. Most doctors ________________ after they learn general medicine.

9b. Some words are ________________ difficult to remember.

10a. Barbara is very ________________ about birds. She knows a lot about them.

10b. The effect that cutting down rain forests will have on the world's climate is ________________.

10c. John would never ________________ hurt his friend's feelings.

H Prepositions

Put a preposition in each blank.

1. People all ______ the world laugh ______ roadrunner cartoons.
2. The roadrunner lives ______ the desert region ______ the United States and Mexico.
3. It spends more time ______ the plants ______ the desert than it does ______ roads.
4. Once ______ a while it eats plants.
5. ______ the spring, a male roadrunner starts looking ______ a mate.
6. Roadrunners can also become friendly ______ people.
7. The birds come one ______ a time and make a noise ______ the window.
8. The bird knocks ______ the window ______ its beak.
9. These birds go right ______ the house.
10. They seem really interested ______ what is happening ______ the program.
11. ______ the winter, nighttime temperatures ______ the desert can be 20°C colder than ______ the day.
12. ______ the early morning, the roadrunner stands ______ its back ______ the sun.

I Connecting Words

Connect a sentence from the first column with one from the second column with **even though**. Write the new sentences on a separate sheet of paper.

1. A roadrunner fits into its environment.
2. The Garbage Project studies landfills.
3. Rain forests cannot support agriculture.
4. The population is increasing rapidly.
5. Women do most of the domestic work.

a. They have 100,000 kinds of plants.
b. It is sometimes dangerous.
c. They work outside the home.
d. Half the world's people have birth-control methods available.
e. It looks funny when it runs.

J Summarizing

Which sentence is the summary?

1. Paragraph 4 (lines 17–22)
   a. It eats a large variety of food.
   b. It eats both plants and meat.
   c. It eats a large variety of food, both plants and meat.
2. Paragraphs 6 through 9 (lines 29–50)
   a. Roadrunners follow people, ask for food, and watch television.
   b. Roadrunners can become friendly with people.
   c. Roadrunners sometimes bring gifts to people.
3. Paragraph 10 (lines 51–63)
   a. Temperatures are much colder at night than during the day.
   b. A roadrunner has an unusual way to keep warm in winter.
   c. A roadrunner collects heat from the sun through a black spot on its back.

K Guided Writing

Write one of these two short compositions.

1. Describe a roadrunner. Include the 3 most interesting things about a roadrunner, in your opinion.
2. Exactly how does a roadrunner fit into its environment?

Afraid to Fly

LESSON

Pre-reading Questions

1. How does this person feel?
2. Have you ever felt like this on an airplane? Describe your experience.
3. Do you know anyone who is afraid to fly?

Context Clues

Circle the letter of the best meaning of the **bold** word.

1. The television program I watched last night was **boring**. It was so slow that I turned it off.

   a. uninteresting　　b. interesting　　c. exciting

2. When the young woman saw Dracula coming toward her, she was **terrified**.

   a. very happy　　b. very frightened　　c. very unhappy

3. Some people are afraid of insects, but most of them can't **harm** you.

   a. hurt　　b. run away from　　c. fly onto

4. After the passengers **boarded** the plane, they put their bags under the seats and fastened their seat belts.

   a. left　　b. saw　　c. got on

5. If you want to buy some stamps, you'd better **rush**. The post office closes in 5 minutes.

   a. walk　　b. hurry　　c. get some money

2

Afraid to Fly

Have you ever flown? Did you fly to another country to study English? How do you feel about flying?

People who have to fly all the time for business usually find it **boring**. People who fly only once in a while are excited. However, some people feel only **terror** when they **board** an airplane. They **suffer** from a **phobia**, an illogical **fear**.

If you are afraid of poisonous spiders, this is logical. If you are afraid of all spiders, even **harmless** ones, this is a phobia because it is illogical. Some people have phobias about **heights**, being shut up in a small area, or being in a large open area. It is not logical to be afraid of these things when there is no danger, but a phobia is not logical.

Fear of flying is another phobia. We always hear about a plane **crash**, but we don't hear about the millions of flights every year that are safe. Riding in a car is thirty times more dangerous than flying, but most of us are not afraid every time we get into a car. It is not logical to be afraid of flying, but research shows that about 12 percent of people have this fear.

People with a phobia about flying are afraid for one or more of these reasons. They are afraid

boring: not interesting

terror = strong fear

board = get on

harmless: not dangerous

heights: noun for *high*

of heights. They **avoid** high places, and if they are in a high-rise building, they don't look out the
30 windows.

They might be afraid of being in an **enclosed** place like an elevator or a **tunnel** on a highway. When they get on an airplane, they can't get out until the end of the flight, and the flight
35 might **last** several hours.

tunnel

Maybe they are afraid of the crowds and all the noise and people **rushing** around at an airport. This especially **bothers** older people.

hurrying

Some people are afraid of the unknown.
40 They don't understand the technology of flying and can't believe that a huge airplane can stay up in the air.

Others are afraid of **loss** of control. They need to control every **situation** they are in.
45 When they drive a car, they have some chance of avoiding an accident. In a plane, they have no control over anything. It **terrifies** them to give up control to the pilot and the rest of the **crew**.

noun for *lose*

verb for *terror*

For some people, a fear of flying is not im-
50 portant because they don't really need to fly. But what about someone who works for an international company? What about an entertainer who has to sing in twenty different places in a month? These people have to fly if they want to continue
55 in their **profession**.

There is help for these people. There are special classes in which people learn how to control their fear. They probably can't lose it, but they can learn to control it. Then they can fly
60 when they need to, even though they probably won't enjoy it.

The class visits an airport and learns how airplane traffic is controlled and how planes are kept in safe condition. A pilot talks about flying

65 through storms, the different noises an airplane makes, and air safety in general. The class learns to do relaxation exercises, and the people talk about their fear.

Next, the class listens to tape recordings of a 70 **takeoff** and landing, and later the people ride in a plane on the ground around the airport. Finally, they are ready to take a short flight.

The **instructors** of these classes are sometimes **psychologists**. They say that between 80 75 and 90 percent of the people who take them are successful. They still have their phobia, but they learn to control their fear. Some of them even learn to enjoy flying.

instructors: teachers

A Vocabulary

terror	height	fear	rush
situation	crew	takeoff	tunnel
harm	board	phobia	enclosed

1. The people who work on airplanes and ships are called the ________________.
2. Tom found himself in a difficult ________________ and he didn't know what to do.
3. A ________________ is an illogical fear of something.
4. ________________ is a very strong word for *fear.*
5. ________________ is the feeling you have when you are afraid.
6. When you are in a hurry, you ________________.
7. Some dogs bite, but most of them won't ________________ anyone.
8. Passengers check in at the airport. Then they ________________ the plane.
9. After ________________, the airplane crew usually brings around drinks and food.
10. Some people become terrified when they are in an ________________ space.
11. What is the ________________ of the tallest building in your city?

B Vocabulary

boring	suffer	tunnels	losses
terrified	profession	bother	psychologist
last	instructor	crash	avoid

1. Many people in Africa ________________ from hunger.
2. Anne was ________________ when she saw a car coming straight at her.
3. What is your ________________? Are you a doctor?
4. Ali's company suffered so many ________________ that he went out of business.
5. An ________________ is a teacher.
6. A plane ________________ usually kills a lot of people.
7. David's composition had very few mistakes, but it was ________________ to read.
8. When you have a cold, try to ________________ giving it to your friends.
9. There are several ________________under the rivers from Manhattan Island to New Jersey and the other parts of New York.
10. Please don't ________________ me now. I'm busy.
11. How long does this class ________________, an hour or less?
12. A ________________ can help you learn to control your fear.

C Vocabulary Review

Cross out the word that does not belong with the other two.

1. stick out, diet, cut down
2. once, couple, pair
3. feather, knock, wing
4. plateau, cloud, mountain
5. even, even though, although
6. often, sometimes, once in a while
7. pollution, surroundings, environment
8. quarter, two-thirds, 40 percent
9. ant, butterfly, bee
10. relatives, females, ancestors

D Multiple Choice

1. ______ usually think flying is boring.
   a. People who fly once in a while
   b. People who fly often
   c. People who have a phobia about flying

2. A phobia is ______.
   a. harmful
   b. illogical
   c. chemical

3. About ______ percent of people are afraid to fly.
   a. 6
   b. 12
   c. 15

4. A person with a fear of enclosed places doesn't like ______.
   a. walking on a path
   b. high places
   c. being in a tunnel

5. ______ especially bother old people.
   a. Crowds at airports
   b. High-rise buildings
   c. Spiders

6. A fear of flying is not important to some people because ______.
   a. they are entertainers
   b. they don't need to fly
   c. they can take a class about flying

7. The instructor of a class for people who are afraid of flying ______.
   a. explains about airplane crashes
   b. learns to relax
   c. takes them to an airport

8. More than _____ percent of people who take these classes are successful.
   a. 12
   b. 80
   c. 90

E Comprehension Questions

1. Have you ever flown? If you have, when was the last time you flew?
2. What are two phobias?
3. Why are we not afraid when we get into a car?
4. Give four reasons people are afraid of flying.
5. Give four examples of people who need to fly.
6. What do people learn in a class for people who are afraid of flying? Tell three things.
7. The class learns how airplane traffic is controlled. How does this help people who are afraid of flying?
8. Why does the class learn about the different noises a plane makes?
9. How do relaxation exercises help the people in the class?

F Main Idea

1. Which sentence is the main idea of paragraph 8 (lines 39–42)?
2. Paragraph 11 (lines 56–61)?
3. Write a sentence for the main idea of the last paragraph.

G Word Forms: Adverbs

Adverbs describe verbs. They also describe adjectives or other adverbs. Many adverbs end in **-ly**, for example, **badly**, and **nicely.** But there are a few adjectives that also end in **-ly**, for example, **friendly** and **lovely**. There are also some common adverbs that do not end in **-ly**, such as **fast** and **hard**.

Please return to the office **immediately**.
Your solution to this math problem is **completely** wrong.

Ali worked **especially** hard today.
Ann is a **friendly** person.
Mike works **hard** at his job.

Sometimes an adverb or an adverbial phrase describes the whole sentence. It is followed by a comma.

Most importantly, you must hand in a report of the meeting by tomorrow morning.
Ordinarily, the class finishes at 2:00. Today it lasts until 2:30 because we have a special lecture.

	Verb	Noun	Adjective	Adverb
1.	poison	poison	poison poisonous	
2.	avoid	avoidance	(un)avoidable	(un)avoidably
3.	bore	boredom	boring	boredly boringly
4.	suffer	suffering		
5.	fear	fear	fearful fearless	fearfully fearlessly
6.	lose	loss	lost	
7.	terrify	terror terrorist	terrified terrifying	

1. Mr. Smith ________________ his rich wife so he could have all her money.
2. It is ________________ for beginning students to make mistakes in English.
3. Students in an English program do not suffer from __________. They are too busy studying. They don't get ________________.
4. There is a lot of ________________ in poor countries.
5. Superman is ________________.
6. The Student Union has a ________________ and Found office. If you are lucky, you might go there and find something that you left in the cafeteria by mistake.
7. Two ________________ hijacked an airplane and made the pilot fly to Paris. The passengers were ________________.

H Articles

Write an article in each blank if one is necessary.

1. _____ people who have to fly all _____ time for _____ business usually find it boring.
2. However, some people feel only _____ terror when they board _____ airplane.
3. They suffer from _____ phobia, _____ illogical fear.
4. If you are afraid of _____ poisonous spiders, this is logical.
5. Some people have _____ phobias about_____ heights, being shut up in _____ small area, or being in _____ large open area.
6. We always hear about _____ plane crash, but we don't hear about _____ millions of _____ flights yearly that are safe.
7. They avoid _____ high places, and if they are in _____ high-rise building, they don't look out _____ windows.
8. They might be afraid of being in _____ enclosed place like _____ elevator or _____ tunnel on _____ highway.
9. When they get on _____ airplane, they can't get out until _____ end of _____ flight, and _____ flight might last several hours.
10. Maybe they are afraid of _____ crowds and all _____ noise and _____ people rushing around at _____ airport.

I Connecting Words

Find a sentence in the second column that goes with a sentence in the first column. Connect the two sentences with **and, but**, or **even though**. Use a comma before **and** or **but**. Write the sentences on a separate piece of paper.

1. Businesspeople are bored with flying.	a. She was a Victorian woman.
2. A roadrunner fits well into its environment.	b. It looks funny.
3. Kingsley traveled in West Africa by herself.	c. Amundsen had arrived there first.
4. The boat was caught in a bad storm.	d. People who don't fly very often find it exciting.

5. Scott reached the South Pole. — e. It sank.

J Summarizing

Write a sentence to summarize each of these paragraphs. Number 2 will have a long sentence. Write a sentence with only the most important idea for numbers 1 and 3.

1. Paragraph 3 (lines 10–17).
2. Paragraphs 5, 6, 7, 8, and 9 (lines 26–48).
3. Paragraph 10 (lines 49–55).

K Guided Writing

Write one of these two short compositions.

1. Do you have any phobias? Describe one. If you wanted to control it, how would you do it?

2. Describe the most terrifying trip you have ever taken, on an airplane or any other kind of transportation.

What Is Jazz?

LESSON

Pre-reading Questions

1. Have you ever listened to a band like this? Where? Did you enjoy the music?
2. Do you play a musical instrument?
3. Do you read music?

Context Clues

Circle the letter of the best meaning of the **bold** word.

1. The president has to **analyze** the situation carefully before he can make a decision, so he needs to get every piece of information that he can.
   a. think carefully about every detail of a situation
   b. get a general idea of the main situation
   c. find out why something happened

2. Thomas Edison **invented** the electric light.
   a. figured out
   b. discovered
   c. made the first one

3. A journalist **interviewed** a couple who feed a roadrunner. After she had talked to the couple, she wrote an article about the interview for a magazine.
   a. asked someone questions on a subject
   b. gave a lecture
   c. went to visit

4. My neighbor's child says he did not take the money that was on my table. I believe him because he is very **honest**.
   a. usually tells the truth
   b. doesn't usually steal
   c. tells the truth and never steals

5. It is hard to stay **calm** when your basketball team needs only one point to win and there are just thirty seconds left in the game.
   a. unexcited
   b. complicated
   c. explosive

3

What Is Jazz?

Paul Giroux is a musician and teacher. The author asked him to **analyze** the interesting subject of **jazz** in an **interview**. In this report of the interview, N.N. **stands for** the author's name, and P.G. are Mr. Giroux's **initials**.

N.N.: Before we talk about jazz, what is music?

P.G.: Music is sound as organized by ordinary people, **folks** like you and me. We describe music using words like **rhythm**, **pitch**, volume, and kind of sound.

N.N.: You used the word "folks." What is "folk" music?

P.G.: I agree with the great jazz **trumpeter** Louis Armstrong, who said, "All music is folk music. I haven't ever heard a horse sing a song."

trumpet

N.N.: (Laughing) Well, then, what is "jazz"?

P.G.: We'll get to that soon. First, we need to define those musical words. Rhythm is the feeling in the body when you hear the regular, strong beat of music, such as a **drum** beat. You tap your foot or clap your hands when listening to a band, or you dance. Folks were dancing long before any history was written. Even dogs and horses dance to musical beats. Pitch is high or low. Women's voices are high. Men's are low. Volume is loud or

drum

soft. The kind of sound comes from the **instrument** used. We blow into wind instruments like the trumpet. We use our hands and fingers on the **violin** or guitar. We hit the drum, the **cymbal**, 30 and the **piano**.

N.N.: When did people start to make music?

P.G.: No one knows. Maybe a mother's soft sounds to her baby became a song. Maybe a hunter's cries became a song. Scientists have 35 discovered bone trumpets which were made very long ago. Ancient fighters in the Middle East made trumpets out of sheep's **horns**. In India and Africa, and also among Native Americans, distant tribes talked to each other by drum beats, 40 which soon became dance music. In China, Turkey, and ancient Rome, groups walked together using the rhythmic beat of cymbals. Cymbals and drums are in all concert and dance bands. Long ago in West Africa, village musicians hit pieces of 45 wood which were pitched from high to low. They named this instrument the *malimba*. Americans said that word incorrectly, so it became *marimba*.

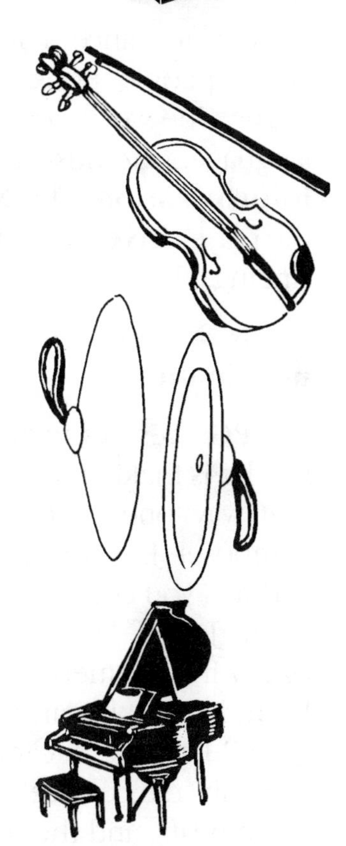

violin, cymbal, piano

horn

N.N.: Isn't that what Lionel Hampton played?

50 P.G.: No, not exactly. Hampton played a newer form of it called the *vibraphone*. Lionel Hampton was **hired** by Benny Goodman in 1936 and in this way became the first African-American to play with a white American group.

55 N.N.: Wasn't Lionel Hampton a jazz musician?

P.G.: Yes, he was.

N.N.: Then that brings us back to jazz?

P.G.: It surely does. As Quincy Jones, another African-American musician, said in 1993, "Jazz is 60 more than just music. It's a feeling." Jazz makes

us want to dance. For a long time in the United States, people thought jazz was not **respectable** music. The word *jazz* comes from a West African language. Jazz music has interesting rhythms and 65 **improvisation**. That word means playing music the player **invents**, or makes up, while playing or singing.

N.N.: Do you mean that the player uses **imagination**?

70 P.G.: Yes. **As long as** the player is improvising, he is making up jazz. If we understand jazz in that way, one of the great jazz players was the composer J. S. Bach more than 300 years ago. Perhaps you could listen to a recording of Bach's 75 "Jesu, Joy of Man's Desiring." About 100 years ago, African-Americans in New Orleans in the United States began to play in a way called *rag-time.*" Ragtime became mixed with Irish songs, Scottish dances, religious music, and African 80 drum beats, and the result was jazz. Musicians in France in the early 1900s used jazz in their music. Maybe you could listen to a recording of the French composer Debussy's "Golliwog's Cake-walk."

if, also *while*

85 N.N.: When did jazz become popular in the United States?

P.G.: It became popular about 10 years before World War II. And after that war, in the 1950s, Benny Goodman was playing jazz to large crowds 90 in Tokyo, Bangkok, Singapore, and Hong Kong.

N.N.: Was Duke Ellington playing in New York at that same time?

P.G.: Yes, and for many years before.

N.N.: What can you tell us about Duke 95 Ellington?

P.G.: Like Lionel Hampton and Quincy Jones, Duke Ellington was an African-American musician. The Duke **honestly** said he was not a jazz musician but a piano player. Much of his music is
100 not for dancing.

honestly: with truth

N.N.: Does the **character** of jazz change with the player?

P.G.: Yes, some jazz is exciting. We call it *hot*. Another kind of jazz is cool and **calm**.

calm: not excited or angry, peaceful

105 N.N.: Is jazz, then, an **original** American art form?

P.G.: Yes, it is. Jazz music has gone from the United States to all over the world. Musicians from many other countries are bringing their own
110 ideas of jazz music to the United States. For example, in the early 1990s, a jazz group from England called the Bluesbreakers was playing in the United States. Also, from East India, Ravi Shankar, a musician who improvises on an East
115 Indian guitarlike instrument called a *sitar,* plays in the U.S. In Beijing, Cairo, Tel Aviv, Cape Town, Istanbul, Bombay, Manila—almost everywhere, it is easy for the traveler to find a jazz club for dancing.

A Vocabulary

honestly	drums	horns	respectable
jazz	analyze	interviews	initials
character	pitch	improvised	original
volume	rhythm	pollution	waste

1. The ________________ of the authors of this book are P.A. and N.N.
2. Your idea is ________________. No one ever thought of it before.
3. Companies try to hire people who work ________________. They try to hire people with a good ________________.
4. Ahmed needed to fix his car in a hurry, but he didn't have exactly the right equipment, so he ________________.
5. I can't sing that part because my voice is too low. Let Flo sing it. Her voice has a higher ________________.
6. All rock bands have ________________.
7. Television news programs often have ________________ with famous people.
8. Camels do not have ________________.
9. Dr. Gomez will use her computer to ________________ her research.
10. My father plays in a ________________ band.
11. No ________________ person would go to that terrible place.
12. Please turn down the ________________ on the TV. I'm talking on the telephone.

B Vocabulary

stand for	folk	trumpet	calm
instrument	invented	violin	cymbal
as long as	hire	imagination	piano

1. A guitar is a musical ________________.
2. You play a ________________ by hitting it with a stick.
3. Some people will travel anywhere ________________ they don't have to fly.
4. Most people have to sit down when they play the ____________.
5. Ms. Davis tried to stay ________________ even though she was very worried about her daughter.

6. Sometimes in the army, soldiers wake up to the sound of a _______________ or bugle.
7. What does U.S. _______________? The United States.
8. The Bakers are going to _______________ someone to do their domestic work.
9. The person who _______________ the typewriter had a wonderful idea.
10. A _______________ looks a little like a guitar.
11. Children use their _______________ when they play.
12. A "_______________ tale" is a story that people in a country or area have told to their children for hundreds of years.

C Vocabulary Review

branches	level	root	earthworms
stretch	glue	moisture	nutrients
flies	direct	explosion	peaceful
spot	snakes	whistle	gift

1. I have to _______________ these papers together.
2. It bothers me when _______________ come around the food at a picnic.
3. Some _______________ are poisonous. _______________ are not, even though they have a similar shape.
4. Maria is at the highest _______________ in the English program.
5. When we eat a carrot, we are eating the_______________ of the plant.
6. Some food provides more _______________ than other food.
7. Leaves grow on the _______________ of trees.
8. Some people can _______________ songs very well.
9. Desert animals don't drink much water. They get it from the _______________ in plants.

D True/False/Not Enough Information

_______ 1. The character of jazz changes with the player.
_______ 2. A music analyst can tell one kind of music from another.
_______ 3. Sounds need organization by people to become music.
_______ 4. Animals can feel drum beats in their bodies.

_______ 5. When a car starts slowly and goes faster and faster, the pitch of the sound it makes goes from high to low.
_______ 6. A fire alarm makes a high-volume sound.
_______ 7. A long time ago, people made musical instruments out of animal parts.
_______ 8. Lionel Hampton, Quincy Jones, Benny Goodman, and Duke Ellington are names of famous jazz musicians.
_______ 9. A jazz musician must play the music exactly as it is written on the paper, the same every time.
_______ 10. Hot jazz and cool jazz are different in character.

E Comprehension Questions

1. Explain three words we use to describe music.
2. What does *imagination* mean?
3. How does Quincy Jones explain jazz?
4. What is a marimba?
5. Where did the word *jazz* come from?
6. Where did people first play "ragtime" music?
7. What musical instrument did Duke Ellington play most?
8. What is the difference between hot jazz and cool jazz?
9. What is the most important characteristic of jazz?
10. Where can you go to hear jazz today?

F Paraphrasing

Use your own words to say the same ideas as these sentences from the text. It is not necessary to use the same number of sentences. You may use more.

1. Music is sound as organized by ordinary people, folks like you and me.
2. As long as the player is improvising, he or she is making up jazz.

G Main Idea

1. Write a sentence for the main idea for lines 32–48.
2. Write a sentence for the main idea for lines 107–119.

H Scanning

1. We blow into ________________ instruments.
2. Lionel Hampton played the ________________.
3. Benny Goodman hired Lionel Hampton in ________________ (what year?).
4. ________________ wrote "Golliwog's Cakewalk."

I Word Forms: Active and Passive

The passive is formed with **be** and the past participle. In an active sentence, the subject performs (does) the action.

The **interviewer** asked several questions.

In a passive sentence, the subject receives the action. Sometimes the person (the agent) who performed the action is included in the sentence after the word **by**. The agent is not included if it is unknown or unimportant. Sometimes everyone knows who the agent is, so it is not necessary to name it.

Several **questions** were asked by the interviewer.
My **car** was stolen last night. (I don't know who stole it.)
Society is studied so that **it** can be better understood. (The people who study society are not important in this sentence.)
Cars are made in factories. (Everyone knows they are made by people.)

Write the correct word form in the blanks, including active and passive forms.

	Verb	Noun	Adjective	Adverb
1.	instruct	instruction instructor	instructive	
2.		(dis)honesty	(dis)honest	(dis)honestly
3.	systematize	system	(un)systematic	(un)systematically
4.	imagine	imagination	(un)imaginative	(un)imaginatively
5.	invent	invention inventor	inventive	
6.	interview	interview interviewer		

7. characterize	character characteristic	(un)characteristic	(un)characteristically
8.	psychology psychologist	psychological	psychologically
9. beg	beggar		
10. depend (on)	dependability	(un)dependable	dependably

1a. The lecture on safe driving was very ________.
1b. The students ________ to arrive on time the first day of classes.
2. ________ is an important characteristic for someone working in a bank.
3. Pat organizes her work ________. She can do more work in less time when she ________ it.
4. That mystery program was very ________. I didn't know how it was going to end until the last minute.
5a. A computer programmer has to be ________ in order to write a good computer program.
5b. The telephone ________ by Alexander Graham Bell.
6. The Minister of Health didn't like some of the questions that the ________ asked him. He ________ by a foreign journalist.
7. Marge started a fight with her sister. This was very ________ of her because she is usually nice to her.
8. Barbara is going to study ________. Then she will work with people who have ________ problems.
9. Dan ________ his friend to lend him his car.
10. Mr. Thompson is a ________ person. You know he will do what he says. You can ________ him.

J Noun Substitutes

What does each noun substitute stand for?

1. page 142 line 2 **him** ________
2. line 6 **we** ________
3. line 17 **that** ________
4. page 143 line 45 **they** ________
5. line 47 **it** ________
6. line 51 **it** ________

7. line 56 **he** ________________
8. page 144 line 81 **their** ________________
9. page 145 line 103 **it** ________________
10. line 109 **their** ________________

K Articles

Write an article in each blank if one is necessary.

1. Paul Giroux is ______ musician and teacher.
2. ______ author asked ______ him to analyze ______ interesting subject of jazz in ______ interview.
3. In ______ report of ______ interview, N.N. stands for ______ author's name and ______ P.G. are ______ Mr. Giroux's initials.
4. I agree with ______ great jazz trumpeter Louis Armstrong, who said, "All ______ music is ______ folk music. I haven't ever heard ______ horse sing ______ song."
5. Rhythm is ______ feeling in ______ body when you hear ______ regular, strong beat of ______ music, such as ______ drum beat.
6. ______ kind of sound comes from ______ instrument used.

L Two-Word Verbs

pick someone up—go somewhere with your car and get someone
stand for —for example, U.S. stands for the United States
see off —go with someone to the airport, for example, when he or she is going to leave
clean up —clean the house after a party, for example, or after some children had a lot of toys out
help out —help

1. UN ________________ the United Nations.
2. Tom had a big party. Afterwards, he had to ________________ the house. Three of his friends stayed to ________________.
3. Ali studied at New York University for 5 years. When he left, twenty people went to the airport to ________________ him ________________.
4. Let's go to the party together. I'll ________________ you ________________ at 9:00.

M Guided Writing

Write one of these two short compositions.

1. Compare jazz with another kind of music you like. How is it the same? How is it different?
2. Describe the music of your country. Tell a little about the history, the instruments, the sound, and the famous musicians.

Skyscrapers

LESSON

Pre-reading Questions

1. **What city is this?**
2. **How tall is the tallest building in your country? How old is it?**
3. **Do you enjoy going up to the tops of tall buildings?**

Context Clues

1. New York City is famous for its **skyscrapers**. They reach up into the sky.

   a. art museums b. wide streets c. tall buildings

2. Carol is only 8 years old, but she loves to draw buildings. She wants to be an **architect** when she grows up.

   a. an artist
   b. a person who plans new buildings
   c. an engineer

3. Mr. Smith is a **pleasant** instructor. He is friendly and helpful to all his students and to the other instructors.

   a. nice b. busy c. new

4. Research shows that seat belts help **prevent** serious injuries in accidents.

   a. stop something before it happens
   b. have fewer accidents
   c. hold the person in the seat

5. In the modern world, people **communicate** by telephone, radio, television, and computer.

   a. talk to each other
   b. give and receive information
   c. get the world's news

4

Skyscrapers

When people think of **skyscrapers**, they think of New York, a city with many high-rise buildings. There is no other city like New York, and this is because of its great buildings that reach up into the sky.

It comes as a surprise then to learn that Chicago, not New York, is the home of the skyscraper. The first high-rise building was built in Chicago in 1884, and it was nine **stories** high. This is not tall **compared** with today's buildings, but it was the first building over six stories. There were no tall buildings before that because the needed technology didn't **exist**.

floors

For centuries, the tallest buildings were made of stone. The lower walls had to be thick enough to support the upper ones. If the building was very high, the lower walls had to be very thick.

Early in the nineteenth century, engineers developed **iron frames for bridges**. In the 1880s, **architects** started using iron and steel frames to support the walls of buildings. The buildings did not need thick walls to hold up the upper stories, so the buildings could be much taller.

people who design buildings

There were other **advantages** to these steel frames. The building walls were thinner and could have more windows, which made the rooms much **pleasanter**. With thin lower walls,

pleasant = nice

there was room for stores and offices on the ground floor. It was also faster to build with an iron and steel frame than with stone.

However, there was still one problem. How would people get up to the top stories in a ten-story building? We all know what the solution was—the elevator. Elisha Otis invented the elevator and first showed it to the **public** in 1853. By the 1880s, there were elevators run by electricity which were fast and light enough to use in skyscrapers. They were developed at just the right time.

There were other problems that architects and engineers who built high-rise buildings had to solve. They had to figure out a way to get water to all the floors. They had to **prevent** the buildings from moving in the wind. **In addition**, they wanted to make them as beautiful as possible. (and)

At the time that architects first started **designing** and building high-rise buildings, thousands of **immigrants** were entering the United States from Europe. They all needed a place to live. Cities were growing fast, and tall buildings meant that many more people could live in a small area, so people started building skyscrapers in cities across the United States.

Over the years, the problems **connected** with high-rise buildings were solved. Buildings got taller and taller. In 1909, a fifty-story building was built in New York, and in 1913, one with sixty floors. In 1931, the Empire State Building in New York was finished; it was 102 stories high. This was the tallest building in the world until 1970, when the World Trade Center was built, again in New York. It has 110 floors. Then the Sears Building was built in Chicago in 1974. It also has 110 stories, but it is taller than the World Trade Center.

Other countries were building skyscrapers too. In Europe, the centers of many cities were

destroyed by **bombs** during World War II. The city planners rebuilt many of the buildings exactly
70 as they had been. In addition, they included high-rises in their plans. Most European cities today are a **mixture** of old and modern buildings.

Tokyo did not have tall buildings for a long
75 time because of **earthquakes**. Then engineers figured out how to keep a high-rise standing during an earthquake. Today there are many tall buildings in Tokyo. In fact, there are tall buildings in cities throughout the world. As the population
80 of cities increases, the number of high-rises increases because they take less space.

movements of the earth

And what about the future? Architects say there is no limit to the height a building can be. An engineer in New York is designing a 150-floor
85 building. An architect in Chicago has drawings of a 210-story building.

We have the technology for these buildings, but do we need them or want them? With the invention of computers, a company doesn't need
90 to have all its offices in one huge building. People can **communicate** by computer from offices **spread** out all over the city, or even from their homes. And do we want 200-story buildings? Do people want to work and live that far above the
95 ground? A skyscraper can be dangerous in a fire, or if somebody puts a bomb in one. The architects and engineers who are planning these new skyscrapers have to think about these questions, or they may build buildings that no one will use.

exchange information

A Vocabulary

skyscraper	advantages	frame	prevent
immigrants	designs	communicate	exist
compare	pleasant	in addition	connects

1. When we ________________ Canadian and American English, we see that there are not many differences.
2. There are many ________________ to learning English because it is an international language.
3. A high-rise building is also called a ________________.
4. A driveway ________________ the garage with the street.
5. Thousands of ________________ arrive in Australia from Asia and Europe every year.
6. It is possible to ________________ many forest fires that people start.
7. In some skyscrapers, the walls are made of a steel ________________ and glass.
8. An architect ________________ buildings.
9. Music has rhythm. ________________, it has pitch, volume, and sound.

B Vocabulary

pleasant	mixture	bomb	spread
exist	architect	story	earthquake
advantage	communicate	prevent	public

1. Hot chocolate is a ________________ of chocolate, sugar, and milk.
2. We've had ________________ weather lately. It has been warm and sunny.
3. In the future, we will ________________ with computers even more than we do now.
4. An ________________ in Turkey destroyed several villages.
5. Dinosaurs do not ________________ anymore.
6. A famous ________________ designed the whole city of Brasilia.
7. The children ________________ their toys all over the floor and then went to watch television.
8. Another word for the floor of a building is ________________.
9. The lecture on modern architecture tonight is open to the ________________. Anyone can go.
10. There was an explosion because of a ________________.

C Vocabulary Review

Match the words with the definitions.

1. colony ______________________
2. interior ______________________
3. border ______________________
4. delay ______________________
5. blind ______________________
6. superior ______________________
7. escape ______________________
8. hemisphere ______________________
9. ashore ______________________
10. blizzard ______________________

a. better
b. half of the earth
c. get away from
d. a place that belongs to another country
e. to the shore
f. line between two countries
g. can't see
h. remote
i. inside
j. sled
k. bad winter storm
l. wait

D Multiple Choice

1. The first skyscraper was built in ______.
   a. Chicago b. New York c. Tokyo
2. Skyscrapers did not exist before 1884 because ______.
   a. steel did not exist
   b. people didn't have the necesssary technology
   c. there were not enough immigrants to live in them
3. Architects got the idea of using iron and steel frames for buildings from ______.
   a. engineers b. other architects c. designers
4. A building with a steel frame does not need ______.
   a. technology
   b. thick walls
   c. stores and offices on the first floor

5. The first building with sixty floors was built only ______ years after a fifty-story building.
   a. 1913 b. four c. eighteen

6. As population increases, ______ increases.
   a. immigration
   b. the number of skyscrapers
   c. the number of old buildings

7. A Chicago architect has designed a building with ______ stories.
   a. 115 b. 150 c. 210

E Comprehension Questions

1. Why is it a surprise to find out that the first skyscraper was in Chicago?
2. Why don't buildings with steel frames need thick lower walls?
3. Name an advantage of buildings with thin lower walls.
4. Why does the text say that elevators were invented at just the right time?
5. What effect did the arrival of thousands of immigrants to the U.S. have on skyscrapers?
6. What is the tallest building in the world today?
7. What is the advantage of high-rise buildings over lower buildings?
8. Why can Japan have skyscrapers today when it couldn't before?
9. Do you think people would use 200-story buildings? What is your reason?

F Main Idea

1. Which sentence gives the main idea in paragraph 2 (lines 6–13)?
2. Paragraph 12 (lines 82–86)?
3. Write a sentence that gives the main idea in paragraph 6 (lines 32–40).
4. Write a sentence that gives the main idea of the last paragraph.

G Word Forms

These are some common verb prefixes and suffixes.

en- —encircle, enclose
-en —darken, shorten
-ize —memorize, colonize

	Verb	Noun	Adjective	Adverb
1.	compare	comparison	comparative	comparatively
2.	please	pleasure	(un)pleasant	(un)pleasantly
3.	add	addition	additional	additionally
4.	(dis)connect	(dis)connection	(dis)connected (un)connected	(dis)connectedly
5.	mix	mixture		
6.		(dis)advantage	(dis)advanta- geous	(dis)advanta- geously
7.	prevent	prevention	preventive	
8.	immigrate	immigration immigrant		
9.	popularize	popularity	popular	popularly
10.	enclose	enclosure		
11.	strengthen	strength	strong	strongly

1a. Spanish spelling is ________________ easy to learn.
1b. By ________________, English is more difficult.
2. It was a ________________ to meet you.
3. People who are afraid to fly don't like being closed in. ________________, they sometimes fear heights and don't understand the technology of flying.
4a. What is the ________________ between the changes in the family and woman's place in society?
4b. We had the phone ________________ because we are moving tomorrow.
4c. You can't put a list of ________________ sentences in one paragraph.
5. Students from several countries are ________________ together in one class.
6. It is ________________ to learn English. Are there any ________________ to learning it?
7. ________________ medicine is better than helping people after they are sick.

8. The ________________ office is open from 9:00 to 5:00.
9a. ________________ is very important to teenagers.
9b. Paper handkerchiefs or tissues are ________________ called *Kleenex*. Most people call them that.
10a. The farmer put his sheep in an ________________ for the night.
10b. The university admissions office included several ____________ with the letter to the new student.
11a. Exercise ________________ the muscles.
11b. I agree with you ________________.

H Two-Word Verbs: Review

Put the right words in the blanks.

1. There was a long line waiting to check ________________ at the airport.
2. A large truck broke ________________ on the highway.
3. Alice goes to the gym every weekend to work ________________.
4. Do you have enough money to live ________________?
5. Could you help me ________________ this weekend?
6. Fixing my car turned ________________ an all-day job.
7. Mr. Brown is working too hard and has to slow ________________.
8. Jean had to drop ________________ of school and get a job.
9. Children don't like to put ________________ their toys when they finish playing.
10. Bob was an hour late because he ran ________________ ________________ gas.

I Articles

Put an article in each blank if one is needed.

1. When people _____ think of _____ skyscrapers, they think of New York, _____ city with _____ many high-rise buildings.
2. It comes as _____ surprise to learn that Chicago, not New York, is _____ home of _____ skyscraper.
3. For centuries, _____ buildings were made of _____ stone.

4. How would ______ people get up to ______ top stories in ______ ten-story building?
5. Elisha Otis invented ______ elevator and first showed it to ______ public in 1853.
6. ______ Amazon River is in ______ tropics.
7. ______ people in my class are mostly from ______ Middle East.
8. ______ Bering Sea is in ______ North Pacific Ocean.
9. ______ Lake Superior is between ______ Canada and ______ United States.
10. ______ history of ______ England is complicated.

J Summarizing

Write a sentence to summarize these paragraphs.

1. Paragraph 1 (lines 1–5)
2. Paragraph 2 (lines 6–13)
3. Paragraph 4 (lines 18–24)
4. Paragraph 7 (lines 41–46)
5. Paragraph 8 (lines 47–54)
6. Paragraph 9 (lines 55–65)
7. Paragraph 10 (lines 66–73)
8. Paragraph 13 (lines 87–99)

K Guided Writing

Write one of these two short compositions.

1. Do you think we should continue to build higher and higher buildings? Why or why not?

2. Describe a skyscraper you have seen. Be very specific and give complete details.

Left-Handedness

LESSON

Pre-reading Questions

1. **What are these people doing? What hand are they using?**
2. **Are you left-handed, or is anyone else in your family?**
3. **Can being left-handed have advantages as well as disadvantages?**

Context Clues

Many words have two meanings. What is the correct meaning in these sentences? Circle the letter of the best meaning of the **bold word**.

1. You can take **as long as** you want to do this test. There is no time limit.

   a. if b. as much time as c. a long time

2. Mr. Rossi doesn't have enough wood to finish the table he is making. He has to buy another **board**.

   a. get on a plane b. uninteresting c. flat piece of wood

3. Maria is 10 kilos overweight so she is going to **diet**.

   a. eat less

   b. the food someone eats

   c. what a roadrunner eats

4. Environmentalists **object** to landfills that pollute.

   a. things b. lists c. are against

5. My brother and his wife are having family problems, but they hope they can **work** them **out**.

   a. get exercise b. work hard c. solve

5

Left-Handedness

Are you a leftie? If you are, you are one of millions in the world who **prefer** to use their left hands. There would be millions more left-handed people if their societies didn't **force** them to use their right hands. (5)

like better

To understand left-handedness, it is necessary to look at the brain. The brain is **divided** into two hemispheres. In most right-handers, the left hemisphere is the center of language and logical thinking, where they do their math problems and memorize vocabulary. (10) The right hemisphere controls how they understand **broad**, general ideas, and how they **respond** to the five **senses**—sight, hearing, smell, taste, and touch.

separated, ÷

(15) The left hemisphere of the brain controls the right side of the body, and the right hemisphere controls the left side. Both sides of the body receive the same information from the brain because both hemispheres are connected. However, (20) in right-handed people, the left hemisphere is stronger. In left-handed people, it is the right hemisphere that is stronger.

Different handedness causes differences in people. Although the left hemisphere controls language in most right-handers, (25) 40 percent of left-handers have the language center in the right hemisphere. The other 60 percent use the left side of the brain or both sides for language.

Lefties prefer using not only the left hand. They prefer using the left foot for **kicking** a ball because the whole body is "left-handed."

There is an increasing amount of research on handedness. For example, one psychologist says that left-handers are more likely to have a good imagination. They also enjoy swimming underwater more than right-handers do.

Left-handedness can cause problems for people. Some left-handed children see letters and words **backwards**. They read *d* for *b* and *was* for *saw*. Another problem is **stuttering**. Some left-handed children start to stutter when they are forced to write with their right hands. Queen Elizabeth II's father, King George VI, had to change from left- to right-handed writing when he was a child, and he stuttered all his life.

Anthropologists think that the earliest people were about 50 percent right-handed and 50 percent left-handed because ancient **tools** from before 8000 B.C. could be used with either hand. But by 3500 B.C., the tools, which were better designed, were for use with only one hand. More than half of them were for right-handed people.

The first writing system, invented by the Phoenicians (3000–2000 B.C.) in the Middle East, went from right to left. The Greeks began to write from left to right around the fifth century B.C. because they increasingly believed that "right" was good and "left" was bad. As time passed, more and more customs connected "left" with "bad." This belief is still **common** in many countries today, and left-handed people suffer because of it.

common: ordinary, easy to find

As the centuries passed and education spread to more levels of society, more and more people became literate. As more children learned to write, more of them were forced to write with their right hands. In the United States, some

teachers finally started **permitting** schoolchildren to write with their left hands in the 1930s. In 70 parts of Europe, left-handed children were still forced to write with their right hands in the 1950s. Today in many countries, all children must write with their right hands even though they prefer using their left hands.

75 Some famous people were left-handed. Julius Caesar, Napoleon, Michelangelo and da Vinci (famous Italian artists), and Albert Einstein were left-handed. Alexander the Great (356–323 B.C.) and Queen Victoria of England also were 80 left-handed. So is Prince Charles.

Paul McCartney of the Beatles plays the guitar the opposite way from other guitarists because he is left-handed. Marilyn Monroe, the famous American movie star, was also left-handed.

85 Are you left-handed even though you write with your right hand? Take this test to find out. Draw a circle with one hand and then with the other. If you draw them **clockwise** (the direction the hands of a clock go in), you are probably 90 left-handed. If you draw them **counterclockwise** (in the other direction), you are right-handed. The test does not always work, and some people may draw one circle in one direction and the other circle in the other direction. But don't 95 worry if you are left-handed. You are in good company.

A Vocabulary

divide	broader	backward	stutter
senses	responding	force	prefer
kick	tool	recycle	hired

1. The main streets of a city are ________________ than the side streets. Broadway is a common street name.
2. A left-handed person who is forced to write with the right hand may begin to ________________.
3. A car can go forward and ________________.
4. Players cannot ________________ the ball in basketball.
5. Would you ________________ coffee or tea?
6. A blind person is lacking one of the ________________.
7. Some students are shy about ________________ in class.

B Vocabulary

divided	tools	force	broad
common	counterclockwise	clockwise	permit

1. A mechanic cannot fix a car without ________________.
2. Twenty ________________ by four equals five. ($20 \div 4 = 5$)
3. ________________ means the way the hands of a clock go. ________________ is the opposite.
4. Parents should not ________________ their children to swim in the pool without an adult there.
5. Spiders are ________________ everywhere except at the North and South Poles.
6. Governments cannot ________________ people to limit the size of their family.

C Vocabulary Review

sticks out	male	mates	nests
once in a while	boring	suffer	crash
fear	tunnel	loss	terrified

1. A man is a ________________.
2. In spring, animals search for ________________.
3. Spiders and birds build ________________.

4. A roadrunner's head ________________ straight in front when it runs.
5. The Simplon ________________ goes under the Alps between Italy and Switzerland.
6. Being afraid to fly is an illogical ________________.
7. We heard a loud ________________ and knew that there had been an accident.
8. Some people think baseball is ________________ because it is so slow.
9. Would you be ________________ to meet Frankenstein?
10. Most people only fly ________________.

D True/False/Not Enough Information

_______ 1. Some Eskimos are left-handed.
_______ 2. Most right-handers do calculus with the left hemisphere of the brain.
_______ 3. When people look at a beautiful building, most of them use the right hemisphere of the brain.
_______ 4. The right hemisphere controls the right side of the body.
_______ 5. Most people in the world use the left hemisphere for language.
_______ 6. Left-handedness can cause children to see letters backwards.
_______ 7. It is easier to write from left to right.
_______ 8. Left-handed people are more intelligent than right-handers.

E Comprehension Questions

1. What does the right hemisphere of the brain control?
2. Which hemisphere is stronger in left-handed people?
3. Why do lefties prefer to kick with the left foot?
4. What problems do lefties have in using machines?
5. When do some left-handers start to stutter?
6. Why do anthropologists think the earliest people were equally divided between left- and right-handedness?
7. Why did the Greeks start writing from left to right?
8. What does "you are in good company" mean?

9. How can you tell if a 2-year-old child is left-handed?
10. Are you left-handed?

F Main Idea

1. What sentence is the main idea for paragraph 4 (lines 23–28)?
2. Paragraph 6 (lines 32–36)?
3. Write a sentence for the main idea in paragraph 9 (lines 53–62).
4. Write the main idea of the last paragraph.

G Word Forms

	Verb	Noun	Adjective	Adverb
1.	communicate	communi-cation(s)	(un)communi-cative	
2.	exist	existence	(non)existent	
3.	prefer	preference	(un)preferential	
4.	divide	division	(in)divisible	
5.	force	force	forceful	forcefully
6.			(un)common	(un)commonly
7.	respond	response	(un)responsive	
8.	permit	permission permit	(im)permissible	(im)permissibly
9.		reality	(un)real	really

1a. There have been many wonderful developments in the field of ________________ in the last twenty years.

1b. I tried to get the information from the president's secretary, but he was very ________________.

2. Frank told everyone that he worked for a large company, but the company is ________________.

3a. Professors should not give ________________ treatment to the students they like.

3b. Short jackets, not long coats, are ________________ by skiers.

4. Ten is not evenly ________________ by 3.

5a. Ms. Bush has a very ________________ personality.

5b. John ________________ to leave the university because his grades were so bad.

6. It is ________________ believed that sons are better than daughters.

7. The injured person ________________ to the doctor's treatment. She is well now.

8a. Psychologists say that adults should not accept ________________ behavior from their children.

8b. You cannot build a house in this city without a building ________________.

8c. Smoking ________________ not ________________ in this building.

9. It seemed ________________ to Abdullah that he had finally finished his doctorate degree and was going home.

H Missing Words

Fill in the missing words.

1. If you are, you are one ___________ millions in ___________ world ___________ prefer ___________ use their left hands.
2. ___________ understand left-handedness, it is necessary ___________ look ___________ the brain.
3. The brain ___________ divided ___________ two hemispheres.
4. Both sides of ___________ body receive the same information ___________ the brain because both hemispheres ___________ connected.
5. There is ___________ increasing amount ___________ research ___________ handedness.
6. But ___________ 3500 B.C., the tools, which ___________ better designed, were for use ___________ only one hand.
7. ___________ the centuries passed and education spread ___________ more levels ___________ society, more and ___________ people became ___________.
8. But ___________ worry ___________ you are left-handed. You are ___________ good company.

I Connecting Words

Put **after, before, when, since**, or **until** in the blanks.

1. I'll give you the book ________________ I see you tomorrow.
2. People who are afraid of flying can control their fear ________________ they take a class.
3. The Garbage Project has been in existence ________________ 1973.
4. Toronto knew it had done a good job recycling ________________ the Garbage Project proved the amount of its garbage had become smaller.
5. Sometimes________________ the roadrunner gets a piece of meat, it takes it back to its nest.
6. There were no skyscrapers ________________ 1884.
7. ________________ Burke started across Australia, he organized the expedition.
8. Some left-handed European children were forced to write with their right hands ________________ the 1950s.

J Finding the Reason

Write the reason for each statement.

Statement	Reason
1. Many left-handers have to use their right hands.	
2. For some people, the center of language is in the right hemisphere.	
3. Both sides of the body receive the same information.	
4. Lefties prefer kicking with the left foot.	
5. King George VI stuttered.	
6. Anthropologists think more than 50 percent of people were right-handed by 3500 B.C.	
7. Paul McCartney plays the guitar differently.	

K Guided Writing

Write one of these two short compositions.

1. Write a short history of left-handedness. Start with the earliest people and continue until today.

2. Your 3-year-old child is left-handed. Your friend thinks you should teach the child to use the right hand instead. What are you going to do and why?

Unit 4

Science

Minds are like parachutes. They only function when they are open.
—Sir James Dewar

A seismologist

Biospheres in Space

LESSON

Pre-reading Questions

1. What kind of building is this?
2. Would you like to live in this building if you couldn't come out for 2 years?
3. Do you read stories or watch movies about traveling in space?

Context Clues

Circle the letter of the best meaning of the **bold** word.

1. A computer is a very **complex** machine.
   a. beautiful b. boring c. complicated
2. Ali said he was from Palestine, but he was **actually** born in Qatar.
   a. preferably b. maybe c. really
3. The members of the group **discuss** a protest to get each other's ideas. Then they start planning.
   a. talk about b. prepare c. publish
4. Pierre has studied English for 3 months **so far**. He plans to study for 6 more.
   a. until now b. away from home c. altogether
5. In rain forests, dead plants **create** nutrients for living plants.
   a. take away b. make c. prevent
6. Most children think video games are **fascinating**. They spend hours playing them.
   a. very boring b. very interesting c. unpleasant

1

Biospheres in Space

Is it possible for people to live on another **planet** such as Mars? **Science fiction** stories have told about space colonies for years, but they were possible only in the author's imagination. Now we are **actually** preparing for space colonies. Scientists really **consider** it possible for people to live away from the earth sometime in the future.

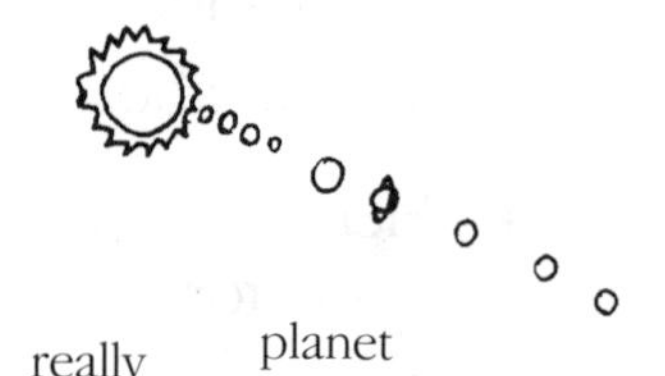

really planet

The Environmental Research Laboratory at the University of Arizona is one of the places that design biospheres (*bio* means *life*, and *sphere* is a *circle*, like a ball) which could be used to colonize other planets. They are very **complex projects**. They are complete, enclosed environments where people can be born, live their whole lives, and die without returning to the earth. There has to be a perfect **balance** among the plants, animals (including humans), and chemical **elements**; that is, among everything in the environment. Specialists on almost everything in our environment, including biologists, biochemists, and people from different areas of agriculture, work on these projects.

complicated

Biospheres might not be round. They could be square or any shape at all. There might be separate **units** for food production. These would be connected to the main unit. Architects and engineers are **discussing** all the possibilities

talking about

now. Scientists have to figure out what shapes biospheres should be, what materials to use, and how small they could be and still support human life.

A greenhouse for growing plants in winter is the first step toward a biosphere. This is a closed environment except for the sun's heat entering through the glass or plastic. Of course, there is a water system from outside, and people bring in nutrients for the plants and take out the waste material. A biosphere will have to have its own system to provide water that can be used and reused. It will need **bacteria** or something else to take care of the wastes. It all must be balanced perfectly, or the whole system will break down.

Nothing enters a biosphere except heat from the sun and information from outside. Biospheres in space will get their information from the earth. Sometimes the information going in and out won't be necessary for the biosphere to exist, but it will be very necessary for research.

The earth itself is the best example of a biosphere. Nothing important enters except sunlight, and nothing leaves as waste except some heat. Everything in the earth's environment has always been balanced, except that now humans are destroying the balance more and more.

We want to build biospheres in space for different reasons. One reason is that there will be a petroleum shortage in the future. Dr. Gerard K. O'Neill, a famous **physicist** from Princeton University, has said that in a few years we will have **satellites** in space to produce **solar** energy and send it to the earth. It will be too expensive to send people and materials continually to the satellites, so biospheres will be necessary. He thinks 10,000 people could live in a space colony sometime in the future. There is another interesting reason to build biospheres. We can use them to

satellite

solar = of the sun

do all kinds of research about our own environment and how it works. By studying biospheres,
70 we can understand better what will happen as humans destroy tropical forests, as we **create** (make) more **carbon dioxide** (CO_2) by burning fuel, and as we pollute the oceans and the air. The information we get from biospheres may keep us
75 from destroying our own environment.

So far (until now) we have only a few places we call biospheres. One is in Oracle, Arizona, near Tucson and the University of Arizona. Many visitors go to see this biosphere every year. However,
80 some scientists think the Oracle biosphere is not a very scientific project because the people inside the biosphere can get more from outside than sunlight and information. They bring in food and other supplies and change the air. They even go
85 outside for medical treatment. In space, people living in a biosphere could not do this. Another place called a biosphere was created in 1993 near the ocean in Sonora, Mexico. It is a huge, protected area for animals and plants. It is a wonder-
90 ful place for scientific research on the environment, but it is not really a biosphere, either, because it is not enclosed.

Learning how to protect our own environment is the most important thing we can do, both
95 for ourselves and for our children. The world's population is increasing very fast, and we are using up our natural resources fast. We need to do everything we can to save our environment before it is too late. Biospheres are **fascinating** (very interesting)
100 projects. Everyone hopes they will be successful.

A Vocabulary

actual	planet	project	science fiction
solar	satellite	complex	recycle
unit	bacteria	consider	carbon dioxide

1. The earth is a ________________. It is part of the ___________ system.
2. ________________ can cause disease. They also destroy wastes.
3. Tom said his new car cost $10,000, but the ________________ figure was $9,980.85.
4. Julia likes to read ________________.
5. A space colony might be all in one ________________, or it might have separate ones for agriculture.
6. The government has a ________________ to build a dam to store water for agriculture.
7. Another word for complicated is ________________.
8. We must ________________ both the advantages and the disadvantages before we start the project.

B Vocabulary

create	satellite	bacteria	carbon dioxide
so far	discussed	actually	elements
balance	project	physicist	fascinating

1. CO_2 means ________________.
2. Gold (Au), oxygen (O), and uranium (U) are all ______________.
3. Destroying rain forests can ________________ problems for the whole world.
4. The class ________________ how to prepare for the TOEFL exam.
5. ________________ there are no buildings over 110 stories high.
6. A ________________ teaches or does research in physics.
7. Before the large increase in population, there was a ___________ between the needs of the people and what the land could produce.
8. Much international communication is now done by ___________.
9. It is a ________________ experience to live in another country.

C Vocabulary Review

energy	avoided	rush	crew
takes off	board	harmful	phobia
honestly	score	interview	initial

1. Please ________________ this paper so I can show my teacher that you have read it.
2. After people ________________ a plane, it ________________.
3. What was the final ________________ of the game?
4. Sometimes students have to ________________ someone and write a composition about it.
5. Smoking is ________________ to the health.
6. ________________ is produced by burning fuel.
7. If you ________________ through your work, you are likely to make mistakes.
8. Kumiko ________________ giving a speech in class by staying home that day.
9. A road ________________ is repairing the main street where I drive every day.
10. Betty said she ________________ forgot to meet her friend for lunch Sunday.

D Multiple Choice

1. Fiction is ______.
   a. true b. imaginative c. boring
2. Biospheres are complicated projects because ______.
   a. everything must be perfectly balanced
   b. scientists don't know what materials to build them from
   c. people from different professions work on them
3. A biosphere ______ be round.
   a. must b. will c. might
4. Biospheres in space could support ______ people.
   a. two or three b. ten c. 10,000

5. A greenhouse ______.
   a. is a partly enclosed environment
   b. is a biosphere
   c. supports plant life independently

6. ______ might take care of the wastes in a biosphere.
   a. A water system
   b. Balanced nutrients
   c. Bacteria

7. Dr. O'Neill thinks ______.
   a. satellites can produce solar energy
   b. about ten people could take care of a satellite
   c. we need a space colony to study the solar system

E Comprehension Questions

1. Why is it a complex project to create a biosphere?
2. What problems must the architects and engineers consider?
3. How is a greenhouse different from a biosphere?
4. Explain why the earth is a biosphere.
5. How does Dr. O'Neill think we will solve the energy shortage?
6. Why can we learn about our environment from the biosphere?
7. Would you like to live in a biosphere on Mars? Why or why not?

F Main Idea

1. Write a sentence that gives the main idea for paragraph 3 (lines 24–32).
2. Paragraph 6 (lines 50–55).
3. What sentence is the main idea for paragraph 7 (lines 56–75)?
4. Write a sentence for the the main idea of paragraph 8 (lines 76–92).

G Cause and Effect

What is the cause of each of these effects?

	Cause	Effect
1.		People can live their whole lives in biospheres.
2.		The whole system might break down.
3.		The same water must be used and reused.
4.		We will need solar energy.
5.		A biosphere will be necessary to run solar energy satellites.
6.		We create more carbon dioxide.

H Word Forms: Verbs and Nouns

Many English words are used as both a verb and a noun. Use ten of these examples in sentences, using some verbs and some nouns.

Verb	Noun
balance	balance
kick	kick
force	force
design	design
interview	interview
initial	initial
fear	fear
crash	crash
harm	harm
bother	bother
whistle	whistle
knock	knock

I Noun Substitutes

What do these noun substitutes stand for? Sometimes the word isn't in the sentence before.

1. page 178 line 3 **they** ______________
2. line 5 **we** ______________
3. line 12 **which** ______________
4. line 26 **these** ______________
5. page 179 line 31 **they** ______________
6. line 49 **it** ______________
7. line 50 **itself** ______________
8. line 64 **he** ______________
9. page 180 line 74 **us** ______________
10. line 91 **it** ______________

J Articles

Put an article in each blank if one is necessary.

1. ______ Environmental Research Laboratory at ______ University of Arizona is one of ______ places that designs ______ biospheres.
2. ______ science fiction stories have told about ______ space colonies for years, but they were possible only in ______ author's imagination.
3. Now we are actually preparing for ______ space colonies.
4. They are ______ very complex projects.
5. There has to be ______ perfect balance among ______ plants, ______ animals (including ______ humans), and ______ chemical elements; that is, among everything in ______ environment.
6. These would be connected to ______ main unit.
7. ______ greenhouse for growing ______ plants in winter is ______ first step toward ______ biosphere.
8. This is ______ closed environment except for ______ sun's heat entering through ______ glass or ______ plastic.

K Guided Writing

Write one of these two short compositions.

1. Should we build biospheres? Why or why not?
2. You are living in a biosphere on Mars. Describe your life.

Earthquakes

LESSON

Pre-reading Questions

1. **What happened in this picture? Where are the people?**
2. **Have you ever been in an earthquake?**
3. **Can we know when an earthquake will occur?**

Context Clues

1. There are two ways to plant seeds. One is to put each seed in a hole in the ground. The other is to **scatter** the seeds on the ground by the handful.
   a. spread around
   b. push into the ground
   c. plant by machine

2. When you take ice out of the freezer, it **melts**.
   a. gets colder
   b. changes to a gas
   c. changes to water

3. At night, scientists **observe** the stars, the solar system, and other objects in the sky at an observatory.
   a. write about
   b. are tested on
   c. look at

4. The prefix *pre-* means *before*. Scientists want to **predict** disasters.
   a. stop them
   b. protect them
   c. tell people about them before they happen

5. A stone sinks in water. A piece of wood or paper **floats**.
   a. goes to the bottom of the water
   b. rides on top of the water
   c. gets very wet

2

Earthquakes

What causes earthquakes? The earth is formed of **layers**. The **surface** of the earth, about 100 kilometers thick, is made of large pieces. When they move against each other, an earthquake happens. A large movement causes a violent earthquake, but a small movement causes a **mild** one.

layers

not serious

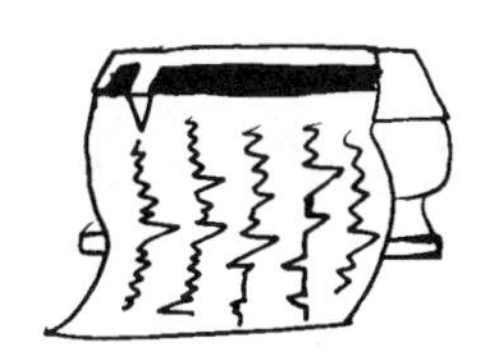

Earthquakes last only a few seconds. The rolling movements are called **seismic waves**. The seismic waves start in one place, called the **epicenter**, and **roll** outward. A seismic wave travels around the earth in about twenty minutes. Usually, an earthquake is strong enough to cause **damage** only near its epicenter.

waves

However, epicenters at the bottom of the ocean create huge sea waves as tall as 15 meters. These waves cross the ocean in several hours. Rushing toward land, they destroy small islands and ships in their path. When they hit land, they **flood** coastal areas far from the epicenter of the earthquake. In 1868, a wave reached 4.5 kilometers inland in Peru. In 1896, a wave in Japan killed 27,000 people.

too much water

After an earthquake happens, people can die from lack of food, water, and medical supplies. The amount of destruction caused by an earthquake depends on where it happens, what time it happens, and how strong it is. It also depends on

types of buildings, soil conditions, and population. Of the 6000 earthquakes in the world each year, only about fifteen cause great damage and many deaths.

In 1556, an earthquake in northern China killed 830,000 people—the most in history. There was no way to measure its strength. In 1935, scientists started using the **Richter Scale** to measure seismic waves. A seriously destructive earthquake measures 6.5 or higher on the Richter Scale.

How can scientists **predict** earthquakes? Earthquakes are not just **scattered** anywhere but happen in certain areas, places where pieces of the earth's surface meet. This **pattern** causes them to shake the same places many times. For example, earthquakes often occur on the west coasts of North and South America, around the Mediterranean Sea, and along the Pacific coast of Asia.

say before it happens

Another way to predict earthquakes is to look for changes in the earth's surface, like a sudden drop of water level in the ground. Some people say animals can predict earthquakes. Before earthquakes, people have seen chickens sitting in trees, fish jumping out of the water, snakes leaving their holes, and other animals acting strangely.

On February 4, 1975, scientists predicted an earthquake in northeastern China and told people in the earthquake zone to leave the cities. More than a million people moved into the surrounding countryside, into safe, open fields away from buildings. That afternoon, the ground rolled and shook beneath the people's feet. In seconds, 90 percent of the buildings in the city of Haicheng were destroyed. The decision to tell the people to leave the cities saved 10,000 lives.

However, more than a year later, on July 28, 1976, the scientists were not so lucky. East of Beijing, Chinese scientists were discussing a possible earthquake. During their meeting, the worst earthquake in modern times hit. Estimates of deaths **ranged** from 250,000 to 695,000. The earthquake measured 7.9 on the Richter Scale.

Earthquakes often come together with volcanic eruptions. In late 1984, strong earthquakes began shaking the Nevado del Ruiz **volcano** in Colombia every day. On November 14, 1985, it **erupted**. A nearby river became a sea of mud that buried four towns. This disaster killed more than 2100 people.

volcano

Mexico City has frequent earthquakes. An earthquake there on September 19, 1985, measured 8.1 on the Richter Scale and killed 7000 people. Most **victims** died when buildings fell on them.

San Francisco, California, also has frequent earthquakes. However, newer buildings there are built to be safe in earthquakes. Therefore, when an earthquake measuring 7.1 on the Richter Scale hit northern California on October 17, 1989, only 67 people were killed. The earthquake hit in the afternoon, when thousands of people were driving home from work. Freeways and bridges broke and fell. Buried under the layers of the Oakland Freeway, people were **crushed** in their flattened cars. Explosions sounded like **thunder** as older buildings seemed to **burst** apart along with the freeways. As the electric power lines broke from the falling bridges and buildings, the sky, covered with huge clouds of black dust, appeared to be filled with **lightning**. Water rushed into the streets from broken pipes and mixed with gas from broken gas lines, causing more explosions.

lightning

Emergency workers had to **cope** with medical problems. Everyone worked together to save

survivors and comfort victims. The next day, the disaster **sites** looked terrible. Victims couldn't find their houses, their cars, or even their streets. Boats were destroyed, and **debris** covered the surface of the sea. There was no water, no electricity, no telephone, only the smell of garbage **floating** in **melted** ice in refrigerators open to the sun. Losses and **property** damage from the earthquake amounted to millions of dollars.

people who did not die
places
garbage

Seismology is the study of earthquakes, and a **seismologist** is a scientist who **observes** earthquakes. Seismologists have given us **valuable** knowledge about earthquakes. Their equipment measures the smallest **vibration** on the surface of the earth. They are trying to find ways to use knowledge about earthquakes to save lives and to help solve the world's energy shortage. The earth's natural activity underground creates energy in the form of heat. **Geothermal** means *earth heat*. This geothermal energy could be useful. However, if we take natural hot water out of the earth in earthquake zones, we might cause earthquakes.

important
movement

People live in earthquake zones because of natural beauty, productive soil, and large existing centers of population. However, people who live there should expect earthquakes. They should be prepared to protect their lives and property. They must build safer buildings and roads. Hospitals and electric power stations must be built as far as possible from probable earthquake sites. When an earthquake starts, people must run to open ground or stay in protected areas like doorways or even bathtubs.

If seismologists could predict earthquakes, we could save about 20,000 human lives each year. Humans can control many things about nature, but we cannot control earthquakes.

A Vocabulary

volcanoes	rolled	floods	valuable
waves	thunder	erupted	damage
patterns	lightning	bursts	melts
float	surface	geothermal	mild

1. Earthquakes happen in ________________ around the world, sometimes several times in the same place.
2. Earthquakes can happen before the eruption of ______________.
3. ________________ energy comes from heat under the earth.
4. Mount St. Helens, a volcano in Washington State in the United States, ________________ in 1980.
5. When Peter set his pencil on the table, it ________________ off onto the floor.
6. When a tire ________________ while a car is moving, it is called a blowout.
7. The weather has been ________________ this week, even though it is winter. It hasn't been very cold.
8. Earthquakes cause a lot of ________________ to towns and roads.
9. Huge ocean ________________ hit the shore during a storm.
10. When there are ________________ and ________________ during a storm, it is sometimes called an electrical storm.
11. Gold and silver are ________________ metals.
12. When snow ________________ in the mountains, it can cause ________________ in the lowlands.
13. There are both heat and activity below the ________________ of the earth.

B Vocabulary

layer	scattered	floating	sites
observe	debris	ranges	seismology
victim	cope	crushed	survivors
vibration	epicenter	property	predict

1. After the huge wave sank the ship, all you could see was some ________________ ________________ on the surface of the sea.
2. The wind ________________ my papers all over the room.
3. In a rain forest, the lower ________________ of plant growth is protected by the upper layer.
4. Students who plan to become teachers usually have to ________________ classes as a first step toward teaching.
5. The freeway bridge fell down because it was near the ________________ of the earthquake. Its weight ________________ people in their cars.
6. When we are standing near a busy freeway, we can feel the ________________ of the traffic under our feet.
7. The yearly pay of an engineer ________________ from $17,000 to $75,000.
8. Before an earthquake, it is difficult to ________________ how many ________________ there will be.
9. Mr. Dahood used to be a rich man, but he was a ____________ of the earthquake and lost all his ________________.
10. Sometimes when people have serious problems, they cannot ________________ with them.
11. ________________ has helped us find possible earthquake ________________.

C Vocabulary Review

For each word in the first column, find a synonym in the second column and an antonym in the third column.

	Synonyms	Antonyms
1. fascinating	a. common	m. uncomplicated
2. complex	b. small	n. excited
3. so far	c. interesting	o. forbid
4. create	d. quiet	p. unusual
5. ordinary	e. complicated	q. boring
6. force	f. make	r. separate
7. broad	g. make someone do something	s. not yet
8. tiny	h. balance	t. actual
9. connect	i. consider	u. narrow
10. calm	j. join together	v. unit
	k. until now	w. destroy
	l. wide	x. huge

D True/False/Not Enough Information

_______ 1. Today scientists know something about the causes of earthquakes.
_______ 2. Earthquakes happen in patterns.
_______ 3. More than half of the world's earthquakes are too small to cause serious damage.
_______ 4. More people are killed by huge sea waves than by buildings falling.
_______ 5. Seismologists can measure the size of seismic waves.
_______ 6. Removing water from the ground causes earthquakes.
_______ 7. Most of the world's earthquakes are mild.
_______ 8. An earthquake in 1989 destroyed the city of Oakland.
_______ 9. People can predict earthquakes by studying the weather.
_______ 10. *Thermal* means *heat*.

E Comprehension Questions

1. How does movement in the earth cause earthquakes?
2. What is the *epicenter* of an earthquake? What is a *seismic wave*?
3. Why does most of the damage from an earthquake happen near the epicenter?
4. Why are earthquakes dangerous when they happen in the middle of the ocean?
5. What do scientists who want to use geothermal energy have to remember about earthquakes?
6. What can you look for to predict an earthquake?
7. What was good about the earthquake that happened in northeastern China in 1975?
8. How can people protect themselves and their property from earthquakes?
9. Why do people continue to live where there are earthquakes?

F Paraphrasing

Use your own words to say the same ideas said in these sentences from the text. It is not necessary to use the same number of sentences. You may use more.

1. Usually, an earthquake is strong enough to cause damage only near its epicenter.

2. The amount of destruction caused by an earthquake depends on where it happens, what time it happens, and how strong it is.

G Main Idea

Write or copy a sentence that is the main idea for these paragraphs.

1. Paragraph 3 (lines 15–23).
2. Paragraph 8 (lines 57–66).
3. Paragraph 10 (lines 74–80).

H Word Forms

	Verb	Noun	Adjective	Adverb
1.	discuss	discussion		
2.	consider	consideration	(in)considerate	(in)considerately
3.		complexity	complex	
4.	fascinate	fascination	fascinating fascinated	fascinatingly
5.	create	creation creativity	(un)creative	creatively
6.	value	value	valuable	
7.	observe	observation observatory	(un)observant	
8.	act	action activity	(in)active	actively
9.	explain	explanation	(un)explainable	
10.	believe	belief	(un)believable	(un)believably

1. After a long ________________, the architects decided to change the design.
2. Marge is a very ________________ person. She thinks of others and what they want, instead of thinking of herself most of the time.
3. The ________________ of modern society affects family patterns.
4. Mark is going to study geology because he is ________________ by rocks.
5. Pablo Picasso was a very ________________ artist. He was known for his ________________.
6. Most people want to have friends. They ________________ the friendship of people they like.
7. When the director of the English program ________________ classes, she writes up an ________________ report.
8. Pierre has become ________________ in the stamp club because he is too busy to attend. Stamp collecting used to be his favorite ________________.
9. Can scientists give a clear ________________ of what actually happens deep in the earth? No, some of the details are ________________ so far.
10. Scientists consider it ________________ that gods create volcanic eruptions.

I Scanning

Scan the text to find this information. Write a short answer and the line number.

1. In 1975, ________________ percent of the buildings in the city of Haicheng were destroyed.
2. Where are some of the places where pieces of the earth's surface meet?
3. The Mexico City earthquake measured ________________ on the Richter Scale.
4. What time of day did the earthquake hit northern California in October 1989?
5. What is the largest number of people killed in an earthquake?

J Two-Word Verbs

Learn these two-word verbs and then fill in the blanks with the right words. Use the correct verb form. Numbers 2 and 3 have the same expression twice.

mix up	—to mistake one thing for another
dress up	—put on special clothes
have on	—be wearing
look out	—be careful
spread out	—spread over a certain area or time

1. Don't try to learn forty irregular verbs in one day. ____________ them ________________ over a week or two.
2. People usually ________________ for a party. Children like to ________________ in their parents' old clothes and play that they are adults.
3. She ________________ her homework assignments and gave the reading homework to the wrong teacher. Then she found out she had done the wrong page. She was ________________.
4. ________________! There's a child in the street!
5. Mike ________________ his running clothes because he was going to exercise.

K Sequencing

Put these sentences about the October 17, 1989, earthquake in the right order. Number 1 is done for you.

_____ a. Freeways and bridges broke and fell.
_____ b. As the electric power lines broke, the dark sky seemed to be full of lightning.
__1__ c. People were driving home in their cars in the afternoon after work.
_____ d. Buildings exploded and pipes broke.
_____ e. Water and gas from broken lines mixed and exploded.
_____ f. The earth began to shake and roll.
_____ g. People died in their cars when the freeways and bridges fell on top of them.
_____ h. Huge clouds of black dust began to cover the sky.
_____ i. Victims could find nothing when they came back.
_____ j. Emergency workers hurried to find survivors and save victims.

L Summarizing

Summarize paragraph 9, lines 67–73. Use your own words to tell the main idea.

M Guided Writing

Write one of these two short compositions.

1. You are in a city when an earthquake hits. Describe what happens. Tell what you feel, see, hear, and smell.

2. You are a seismologist. Tell what scientific information you know about earthquakes. Include how and where they happen and what you are studying right now.

Snow and Hail

LESSON

3

Pre-reading Questions

1. **What is the difference between snow and hail?**
2. **Are there cold storms in the winter where you live?**
3. **Do you like to look at snow? Do you like to be outside in it?**

Context Clues

1. When a violent volcanic eruption **occurs**, there is usually damage.
   a. damages b. scatters c. happens

2. We could not breathe without the earth's **atmosphere**.
   a. the air around the earth
   b. the movement of the earth around the sun
   c. the water on the surface of the earth

3. When Carol is doing research, she often finds useful information in several places in the same book. She puts a **strip** of paper in each place so she can find it again easily.
   a. a large white paper to take notes on
   b. a long, thin piece of paper
   c. a round piece of paper

4. Wheat, corn, cotton, and fruit are valuable farm **crops**.
   a. plants people eat
   b. food that grows on low plants
   c. plants farmers grow

5. One cold January day in Montreal, dark clouds appeared in the sky, the day grew colder, and millions of **snowflakes** began to fall.
   a. pieces of ice b. rain c. pieces of snow

6. The earth is round. This is a **fact**.
   a. true information b. idea c. prediction

3

Snow and Hail

Millions of people in the world have never seen snow. Others see more of it than they want to. Hail is much more common; it **occurs** even in deserts.

happens

5 Each tiny piece of snow is called a **snowflake**, and each flake has six sides or six **points**. Billions of snowflakes fall every winter, and the amazing **fact** is that each one is different. A snowflake is as individual as someone's hand-
10 writing or **fingerprint**.

fingerprint

A snowflake forms inside a winter storm cloud when a **microscopic** piece of dust is **trapped** inside a tiny drop of water. This happens in the **atmosphere** 10 kilometers above
15 the earth. The water freezes around the dust, and as this flake is blown by the wind, it collects more drops of water. These drops freeze too, and the snowflake becomes heavy enough to fall to the earth. As it falls, it passes through areas where
20 the temperature and humidity vary. It collects more and more tiny drops of water, and the shape continually changes. Some drops fall off and start to form new snowflakes.

very small

can't escape

air around the earth

microscope

This sounds simple, but it is actually very
25 complex. It is so complex that mathematicians using computers are just beginning to understand what happens. Every change in temperature and humidity in the air around the snowflake causes a

change in the speed and pattern of the snow-
30 flake's formation as it makes its trip to the earth. Since no two flakes follow exactly the same path to the ground, no two snowflakes are exactly alike. However, they are all six-sided. So far, no one understands why this is **so**.

true

35 Hail is a small round ball of **alternating** layers of snow and clear ice. It forms inside thunderclouds. There are two theories about how hailstones form.

One **theory** says that hail forms when drops
40 of water freeze in the upper air. As they fall, they collect more drops of water, just as snowflakes do. They also collect snow. The ice and snow build up in layers. If you cut a hailstone, you can see these alternating layers.

45 The other theory says that hail starts as a raindrop. The wind carries it higher into the atmosphere, where it gets covered by snow. It becomes heavy and begins to fall. As it falls, it gets a new layer of water, which freezes. Then the
50 wind carries it back up to the snow region, and it gets another layer of snow. This can happen several times. Finally, the hailstone is too heavy to travel on the wind, and it falls to the ground.

Only thunderstorms can produce hail, but
55 very few of them do. Perhaps only one in 400 thunderstorms creates hailstones.

Hail usually falls in a **strip** from 10 to 20 kilometers wide and not more than 40 kilometers long.

a long, thin area

60 A hailstone is usually less than 8 centimeters in **diameter**. However, hailstones can be much bigger than that. Sometimes they are as big as baseballs. The largest ever **recorded** weighed over 680 grams and had a diameter of 13
65 centimeters.

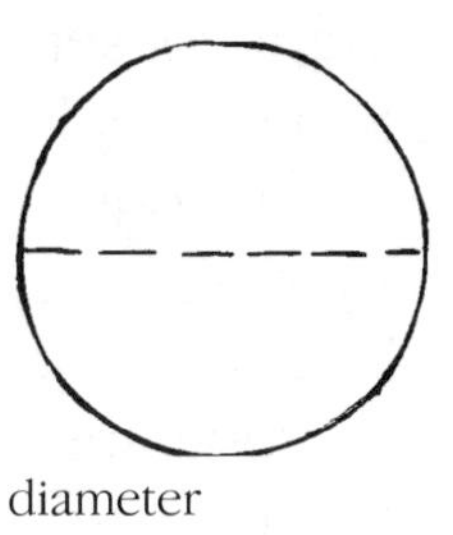

diameter

Hail can do a lot of damage to agriculture, especially since hail usually appears in **mid**summer, when the plants are partly grown. If the **crops** are destroyed, it is too late to plant more, and the farmer has lost everything. The most damage is done by hailstones that are only the size of peas. In one terrible hailstorm in 1923 in Rostov, in Ukraine, twenty-three people and many cattle were killed.

in the middle

Snow can cause damage too. It can cave in the roof of a building. A heavy snowstorm can delay airplane flights and cause automobile accidents. Farm animals sometimes die in snowstorms, and when country roads are closed by the snow, people can be trapped in their cars and freeze to death. Yet there is nothing more beautiful than the sight of millions of snowflakes falling on a still, moonlit night. That is when people think of the beauty, and not the science, of snowflakes.

A Vocabulary

fact	exactly	midsummer	traps
so	records	snowflake	microscopic
alternating	strip	points	fingerprint

1. Hail falls in a ________________ about 40 kilometers long.
2. Volcanoes occur in patterns. This is a ________________.
3. The weather is warm or hot in ________________.
4. Trappers set ________________ to catch animals.
5. Some people still believe that volcanic eruptions are caused by angry gods, but we know this isn't ________________.
6. Every ________________ has 6 sides or 6 ________________.
7. The boys and girls lined up in ________________ rows.
8. Bacteria are ________________. They can't be seen without a microscope.
9. The government ________________ the daily amount of rainfall.

B Vocabulary

occur	fingerprint	fact	atmosphere
theory	hail	so	crop
trap	microscope	diameter	exactly

1. No two individuals are ________________ the same, not even twins.
2. When did the last eruption of Kilauea ________________?
3. The police ________________ criminals.
4. The distance across a circle is called the ________________.
5. Humans are polluting the earth's ________________.
6. Albert Einstein developed a very important ________________ about relativity.
7. Cacao (chocolate) is an important ________________ in West Africa.
8. ________________ can destroy a farmer's crops.

C Vocabulary Review

Match the words with their definition.

1. hire ________________	a. movement of the earth
2. compare ________________	b. look for similarities
3. in addition ________________	c. ÷
4. immigrant ________________	d. pleasant
5. earthquake ________________	e. give a job to
6. story ________________	f. CO_2
7. prefer ________________	g. floor
8. divide ________________	h. frame
9. respond ________________	i. of the sun
10. permit ________________	j. talk about
11. discuss ________________	k. person who goes to another country to live for the rest of his or her life
12. carbon dioxide ________________	l. answer
13. solar ________________	m. like better
14. create ________________	n. allow
	o. and
	p. make

D Short Answers

Write **hail**, **snow**, or **hail and snow** after each of these sentences.

1. As it is blown by the wind, it collects water.
2. It occurs only in the colder regions of the world.
3. It is formed of layers of ice and snow.
4. It can destroy crops.
5. It can cause the death of humans.
6. It is sometimes formed around a piece of dust.
7. It always has six sides or points.
8. It is produced only by thunderstorms.
9. It is a small round ball.
10. It can cause damage.

E Comprehension Questions

1. Why do all snowflakes have six sides or six points?
2. Snowflakes start forming around two things. What are they?
3. What does a change in humidity do to the formation of a snowflake?
4. Why are no two snowflakes alike?
5. Where do hailstones form?
6. What causes both snowflakes and hail to fall to the ground?
7. About how big is the average hailstone?
8. How does hail destroy crops?
9. Give an example of how snow can be destructive.
10. Which is more destructive, hail or snow? Why?
11. Do roadrunners ever see hail?

F Main Idea

1. Write a sentence for the main idea of paragraph 2 (lines 5–10).
2. Paragraph 4 (lines 24–34).
3. Which sentence is the main idea of paragraph 11 (lines 66–74)?

G Word Forms: Negative Prefixes

These are common negative prefixes. Put a word from item no. 1 in the first sentence, and so on. Use the right form of the word.

1. **dis-** dislike, discomfort, displease, disconnect, dishonest
2. **un-** unequipped, uncreative, unprepared, unobservant
3. **non-** nonsmoking, nonalcoholic, nonviolent, nonindustrial
4. **in-** inactive, inconsiderate, incorrect, inexpensive
5. **im-** impossible, improbable, immovable, imperfect
6. **il-** illogical, illiterate
7. **ir-** irregular, irreligious
8. **mis-** misbehave, misspell, misunderstand, misspeak

1. Alice always ________________ the television during a thunderstorm.
2. Bering and his men were ________________ for living on the island after their boat sank.
3. Coke and Pepsi are ________________ drinks.
4. It is ________________ to eat something in front of someone else and not offer them some.
5. It is ________________ to squeeze water out of a stone.
6. It is ________________ to think that someone who is ________________ is unintelligent.
7. ________________ verbs must be memorized.
8. There are three ________________ words in your homework paper.

H Articles

Write an article in each blank if one is needed.

1. _____ snowflake forms inside _____ winter storm cloud when _____ microscopic piece of dust is trapped inside _____ tiny drop of _____ water.
2. This happens in _____ atmosphere 10 kilometers above _____ earth.
3. _____ water freezes around _____ dust, and as this flake is blown by _____ wind, it collects more drops of _____ water.

4. As it falls, it passes through ______ areas where ______ temperature and ______ humidity vary.
5. It is so complex that ______ mathematicians using ______ computers are just beginning to understand what happens.
6. Every change in ______ temperature and ______ humidity in ______ air causes ______ change in ______ speed and ______ pattern of ______ snowflake's formation as it makes its trip to ______ earth.
7. ______ hail is ______ small round ball of ______ alternating layers of ______ snow and ______ clear ice.

I Compound Words

Make compound words using a word from the first column and one from the second.

1. take ______________	a. by
2. blow ______________	b. water
3. thunder ______________	c. storm
4. in ______________	d. walk
5. under ______________	e. off
6. under ______________	f. lands
7. through ______________	g. ground
8. near ______________	h. side
9. side ______________	i. out
10. low ______________	j. out

J Summarizing

Write a summary of the information about snow. Write 5 or 6 sentences.

K Guided Writing

Write one of these two short compositions.

1. Compare snow and hail.
2. Describe a serious winter storm that you have experienced or heard about.

Photovoltaic Cells—Energy Source of the Future

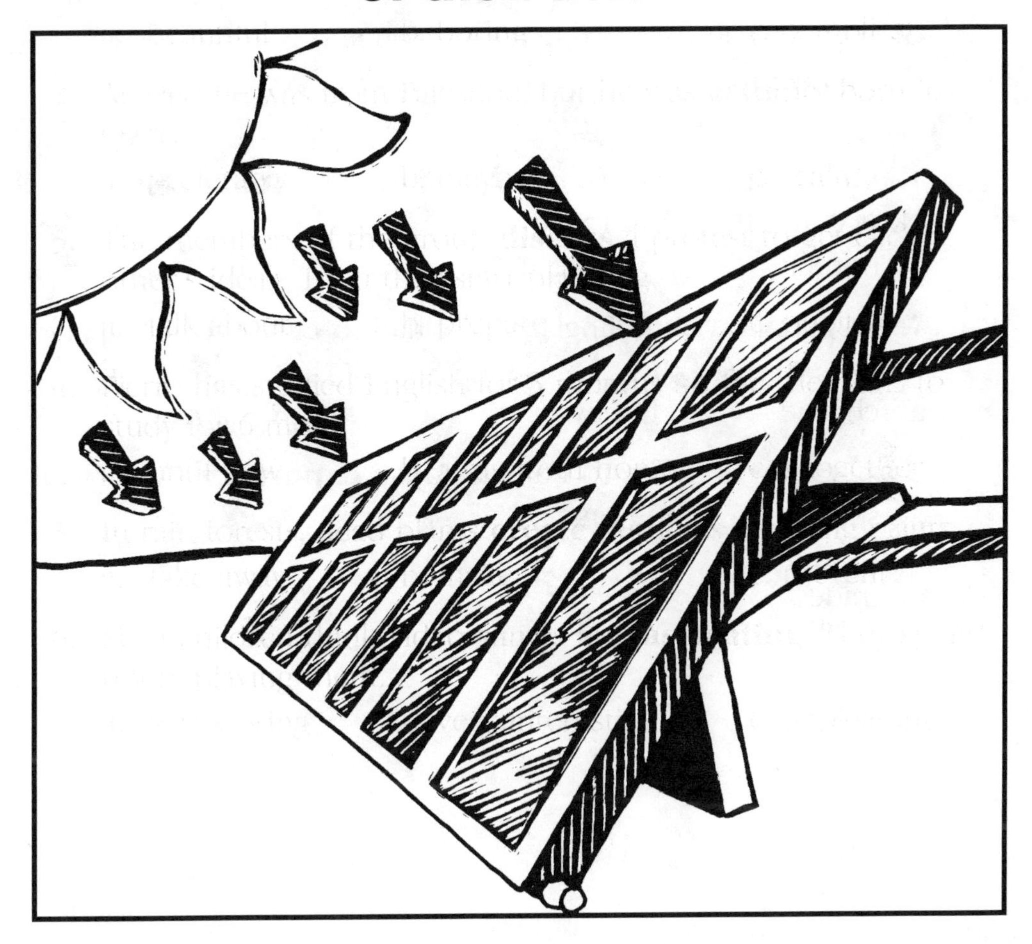

LESSON

Pre-reading Questions

1. What is solar energy?
2. Do you have anything with you right now that works by solar energy? What is it?
3. How do we produce electricity? Name as many ways as you know.

Context Clues

1. The energy from the sun is **inexhaustible**.
   a. very tired b. can never be used up c. never gets tired

2. Glass and water are **transparent**. Iron and wood are not.
   a. expensive b. can float c. can be seen through

3. The Rio Grande River forms part of the **boundary** between Mexico and the United States.
   a. border b. pattern c. highway system

4. When Masako visited England, she had to **convert** her Japanese money into pounds.
   a. change b. buy c. earn

5. Brazil **exports** coffee to Europe. Japan **exports** cars to China.
   a. sells to another country
   b. produces
   c. trades

4

Photovoltaic Cells

As population increases and countries industrialize, the world's **demand** for energy increases. Our supply of petroleum and gas is limited, but the photovoltaic cell offers a solution to
5 the problem of a future energy shortage. This cell is already an important **source** of energy. In fact, it seems almost like **magic**. The photovoltaic cell changes sunlight directly into energy. Solar energy, energy from the sun, is clean, easily avail-
10 able, **inexhaustible**, and free, if the equipment is available.

can't be used up

Did you ever reach to open the door at a store or hotel and see it open by itself? Does your camera always let in the right amount of light for
15 your pictures? These are examples of uses of photovoltaic cells. They are also used in calculators and watches, in remote telecommunication units, and in central power stations to produce electricity. Another important use is in the space
20 exploration program. This program could not exist without the energy produced by photovoltaic cells.

The photovoltaic cell is simple. It has a **transparent** metallic film at the top. Below this
25 is a layer of **silicon** (Si). A metal base is at the bottom.

can be seen through

The sunlight falls on the **boundary** between the two different types of **semiconductors** in

the photovoltaic cell, the silicon and the metal
30 base. A **conductor** is something that electricity can pass through. Water and metals conduct electricity, but wood does not. A semiconductor conducts electricity poorly at low temperatures, but when heat or light is added, conductivity is in-
35 creased.

As the light falls on this boundary between the two types of semiconductors, it creates an electric **current**. The sunlight is **converted** directly into electricity. — changed

40 Another advantage is that this cell is **solid-state**; that is, there are no moving parts. **Since** there are no moving parts to break down, the cell will last a long time if it is protected from damage. This protection is important. If the top of the cell — because
45 even gets dusty, less light enters, and the cell doesn't work as **efficiently** as it should.

In addition, silicon is one of the commonest elements in the world; for example, sand is made up mostly of silicon. However, the chemical prep-
50 aration of the silicon for use in a photovoltaic cell was very expensive at first. A maximum unit of energy cost about $50. Now the cost has decreased to less than $5. Scientists have found a way to produce silicon in long sheets similar to
55 the way plastic for plastic bags is made today. Therefore, the cost of a unit of solar energy will soon fall below $1. Then solar energy will cost the same as usual methods of energy production.

About 18 percent of the sunlight that reaches
60 the cell is converted into electricity. This is a small amount, so many cells must be used to create a **reasonable** amount of electricity. However, technology can be developed to make the cells more efficient and raise this to 27 percent.

65 What does this mean to the world? Photovoltaic cells have several advantages over **fossil** fuels (gas, oil, and coal). Fossil fuels that we use

today were formed from plants and animals that lived millions of years ago. Those plants and
70 animals were able to exist because of the sun. **Obviously**, we can't wait a million years for more fossil fuels. The photovoltaic cell gives us the ability to produce energy directly from the sun. The sun's energy can be converted for our use
75 immediately.

can be seen or understood easily

At the present time, gas and oil are expensive. Developing countries cannot **export** enough agricultural products and other **raw materials** to allow them to **import** the fuel that
80 they need to produce energy. At the same time, petroleum supplies are limited, and in a few decades, they will run out. However, the supply of sunlight is limitless, and most of the poor countries of the world are in the tropics where there
85 is plenty of sunlight.

sell to other countries

The photovoltaic cell has another very important advantage. It is a clean source of energy. The fossil fuels that we use today are the main source of the pollution in our atmopshere.

90 It took only a decade for scientists to learn that solar energy from photovoltaic cells was not just a dream. They have already proven that it can become an important source of energy. By the end of the century, it will be cheaper to produce
95 electricity with solar cells than from petroleum. The photovoltaic cell can be the solution to one of the most serious problems in the world today.

A Vocabulary

photovoltaic cell	inexhaustible	silicon	semiconductors
solid-state	fossil	import	exports
magic	raw material	reasonable	source

1. Scientists think that the ________________ will be an important energy source for the future.
2. The number of snowflakes is limitless and ________________.
3. A photovoltaic cell has two different types of ________________.
4. Petroleum is a ________________ fuel.
5. The ________________ of a river is the place it begins.
6. Children like to see ________________ shows.
7. Japan ________________ television sets but has to ________________ oil.
8. ________________ (Si) is used to make glass.
9. Iron is the main ________________ for making steel.

B Vocabulary

demanded	current	since	efficient
obvious	last	reasonable	transparent
boundary	fossil	conducts	converts

1. Electric ________________ can pass through metal because metal ________________ electricity.
2. The factory workers ________________ higher pay for their work.
3. Much of the ________________ between Canada and the United States is a straight line.
4. Abdullah missed the test ________________ he was late for class.
5. Thirty minutes is a ________________ length of time for a short test.
6. It is ________________ that Carlos copied Maria's homework. The papers are exactly alike.
7. It is more ________________ for thirty people to ride in a bus than in thirty different cars.

8. Glass is ________________.
9. A hydroelectric power station ________________ water power into electricity.

C Vocabulary Review

Underline the word that does not belong with the others.

1. hail, snowflake, trap, rain
2. create, damage, destroy, harm
3. definite, sure, exact, bacteria
4. satellite, planet, star, sun
5. consider, object, discuss, talk over
6. backward, forward, clockwise, sideward
7. physicist, anthropologist, chemist, geologist
8. burst, eruption, flood, earthquake
9. fly, bee, ant, snake

D Multiple Choice

1. Solar energy will not be ______ in the future.
   a. expensive b. easily available c. limitless
2. Sunlight first enters a photovoltaic cell through ______.
   a. a metal base b. a metalic film c. a layer of silicon
3. The place where the two semiconductors meet is called the ______.
   a. border b. conductor c. boundary
4. A semiconductor works best ______.
   a. when there is wood available
   b. when the temperature is low
   c. when light or heat is added
5. A photovoltaic cell ______ light into electricity.
   a. currents b. converts c. conducts
6. The cell must be protected from ______.
   a. dust b. light c. movement

7. At first, these cells were expensive to make because ______.
   a. the chemical preparation of silicon was expensive
   b. silicon is expensive and hard to find
   c. it is hard to keep dirt off the cells

8. Most of today's air pollution comes from ______.
   a. automobiles
   b. burning fossil fuels
   c. factories

E Comprehension Questions

1. Why do we need a new way to produce energy?
2. Describe a photovoltaic cell.
3. Give three advantages of photovoltaic cells over fossil fuels.
4. In what part of the cell is the electric current created?
5. What does *solid-state* mean?
6. What happens when a photovoltaic cell gets dusty?
7. Why was energy from photovoltaic cells expensive in the beginning?
8. How can these cells help Third World countries?
9. Why are photovoltaic cells so important in the space program?

F Main Idea

1. Which sentence is the main idea of paragraph 1 (lines 1–11)?
2. What is the main idea of paragraph 9 (lines 65–75)?
3. Write a sentence for the main idea of paragraph 2 (lines 12–22).
4. Write the main idea of paragraph 6 (lines 40–46).

G Scanning

1. Name a material in the reading that does not conduct electricity.
2. Name a material in the reading that is made mostly of silicon.
3. About how much did a unit of solar energy cost at first? About how much does it cost now?
4. Name three fossil fuels.

H Two-Word Verbs

get in —arrive, for example, a bus or plane
bring up —raise children
show up —appear
stand by —wait for a seat on an airplane without a ticket
leave out—skip, forget to include something

1. When Ali did his homework, he ________________ the third exercise. He forgot to do it.
2. What time does the train from Paris ________________?
3. The airline said there were no seats available on this flight, but if someone doesn't ________________, I can have that seat. I have to ________________ until everyone has boarded. Sometimes standby seats are cheaper, but you take the chance of not getting on the flight.
4. Mary was born on a farm, but she was ________________ in a small town.

I Missing Words

Fill in the blanks with any word that fits in the sentence.

1. ______ population increases and countries industrialize, ______ world's demand ______ energy increases.
2. This cell ______ become ______ important source ______ energy.
3. ______ you ever reach ______ open ______ door ______ a store ______ hotel ______ see it open ______ itself?
4. This program could ______ exist ______ the energy produced ______ photovoltaic cells.
5. It has ______ transparent metallic film ______ the top. ______ this is ______ layer of silicon (Si).
6. The sunlight falls ______ the boundary ______ two different types ______ semiconductors, ______ silicon ______ the metal base.
7. This cell ______ solid-state; ______ is, ______ are no moving parts.
8. Since there ______ no moving parts to break ______, the cell ______ last ______ long time ______ it is protected ______ damage.

9. If ______ top of ______ cell even ______ dusty, less ______ enters, ______ the cell ______ work as efficiently ______ it should.

J Word Forms

This is a common use of an adjective. There are two sentence patterns.

It is + adjective ______________.

It is necessary to memorize irregular verbs.
It is beautiful to walk by the ocean on a moonlit night.

It is important that you fill out these papers immediately.
It is wonderful that you won first place in the competition.

	Verb	Noun	Adjective	Adverb
1.	trap	trap		
		trapper		
2.	alternate	alternate	alternate	alternately
		alternative	alternative	alternatively
3.	occur	occurrence		
4.	bound	boundary	bound	
5.	theorize	theory	theoretical	theoretically
6.		efficiency	(in)efficient	(in)efficiently
7.		reasonableness	(un)reasonable	reasonably
8.	exhaust	exhaustion	(in)exhaustible	(in)exhaustibly
9.		transparency	transparent	transparently
10.	convert	conversion		

1. When an animal is ______________, it can't get away.
2a. There is no ______________ to our plan. We can find no ______________ plan.
2b. The government can give poor people free food or, ______________, it can give them money to buy food.
3. There were three ______________ of breakdown in the electric power station.
4. Norway is ______________ by Sweden, Finland, Russia, the Atlantic Ocean, and the North Sea.
5a. Scientists ______________ about the center of the earth, but they can't know for sure.
5b. ______________, there are black holes in space.

6. It is ________________ to write by hand instead of using a computer.
7. It is ________________ to expect a student to memorize fifty new words a day.
8. Scott and his men became ________________ on their journey back from the South Pole.
9. ________________ is a characteristic of water and glass.
10. Missionaries try to ________________ people to their religion.

K Finding the Reason

Write the reason for each statement.

Statement	Reason
1. The entrance door at a hotel opens by itself.	
2. Electricity can pass through water.	
3. The first photovoltaic cells were very expensive.	
4. These cells can help the Third World.	
5. Energy from the sun is inexhaustible.	
6. The photovoltaic cell can't break down.	
7. The photovoltaic cell might work inefficiently.	

L Guided Writing

Write one of these two short compositions.

1. What are some of the advantages of solar energy over energy made from fossil fuels?
2. What are some of the disadvantages of solar energy?

Biological Clocks

LESSON 5

Pre-reading Questions

1. **Do you get up at the same time on weekends as on weekdays?**
2. **What part of the day do you prefer? In other words, when do you feel best—early in the morning, in the middle of the day, in the afternoon, at sunset, or late at night?**
3. **If you take a long trip on an airplane, do you feel uncomfortable when the time zone changes?**

Context Clues

Circle the letter of the best meaning of the **bold** word.

1. France, England, the United States, Japan, South Africa, and Australia are examples of countries in the two **temperate** zones.
   a. the hot, humid tropics
   b. near the North or South Pole
   c. between the tropics and the Arctic or Antarctic Circle

2. At **dawn** the sky begins to get light and the sun appears.
   a. sunrise
   b. sunset
   c. a storm with thunder and lightning

3. Millions of monarch butterflies **migrate** every fall from North America to southern Mexico and Central America. In the spring, they return north.
   a. travel a long distance because of the season
   b. travel a long distance to lay eggs
   c. return to their home

4. Every night Mohammed sets his **alarm** clock. In the morning, it wakes him up.
   a. a clock that makes a noise at a certain hour
   b. a clock that tells the day, month, and year
   c. a clock that is in the bedroom

5. The private school organized several **events** for Parents' Day. There were races for the small children, a soccer game, a musical program, a picnic, and meetings with the teachers.
   a. any kind of game or sport
   b. anything that happens
   c. programs for children

5

Biological Clocks

If you have ever flown across several time zones, you have **experienced jet lag**. You arrived in a new time zone, but your body was still living on the time in the old zone. You were wide
5 awake and ready for dinner in the middle of the night, and you wanted to sleep all day.

People suffer from jet lag because all living things have a biological clock. Plants and animals are all in rhythm with the natural divisions of
10 time—day and night and the seasons.

At sunrise, plants open their leaves and begin producing food. At night, they rest. In the **temperate** zones of the earth, trees lose their leaves in fall as the days grow shorter and there
15 is less sunlight. In the spring, leaves and flowers begin growing again as the days lengthen.

Rain sets the rhythm of desert plants. Plants in the desert may appear dead for months or even years, but when it begins to rain, the plants
20 seem to come to life overnight. The leaves turn green, and flowers appear. The plants produce seeds quickly, before the rain stops. These seeds may lie on the ground for years before the rain starts the cycle of growth again. The plants' bio-
25 logical clock gave the **signal** for these things to happen.

At **dawn** most birds wake up and start singing. When the sun goes down, they go to sleep.

sunrise

When spring arrives, they start looking for a
30 mate. When winter comes, some birds **migrate** to a region with a warmer climate. Their biological clocks tell them it is time to do all of these things.

Animals that live near the sea and depend on both the land and water for their food have their
35 biological clocks set with the **tides**. When the tide goes out, they know it is time to search for the food that the sea left behind it.

Some insects seem to set their **alarm** clocks to wake them up at night. They are out all night
40 looking for food and then sleep during the day. Honeybees have a very strong sense of time. They can tell by the **position** of the sun exactly when their favorite flowers open.

Some French scientists did an **experiment**
45 with honeybees. They put out sugar water every morning at 10:00 and at noon, and the bees came to drink the water at exactly the right time. Then the scientists put the sugar water in a room that was brightly lit twenty-four hours a day. They
50 started putting the sugar water out at 8:00 p.m. It took the bees a week to find it at the different hour, but from then on, they came to eat in the evening instead of in the morning.

Later the scientists took the honeybees to
55 New York. The bees came for the food at the time their bodies told them, only it was 3:00 p.m. New York time. Their bodies were still on Paris time.

Humans, like other animals, have a biological clock that tells us when to sleep and eat. It causes
60 other changes too. Blood **pressure** is lower at night, the **heartbeat** is slower, and the body temperature is a little lower. We even go through several levels of sleep, cycles of deep and light sleep.

Other **events** occur in cycles too. More ba-
65 bies are born between midnight and dawn than at any other time. More natural deaths occur at night, but more heart **attacks** happen early in

events: anything that happens

the morning. Most deaths from diseases in hospitals occur between midnight and 6:00 a.m. 70 Some police say there are more violent crimes and traffic accidents when there is a full moon.

The honeybees in the experiment reset their biological clock for different feeding hours. Humans do this too. People who work at night learn 75 to sleep during the day and eat at night. Students who fly halfway across the world to study in another country get used to the new time zone after a few days. When they go home, they change back again. Our bodies are controlled by 80 a biological clock, but we can learn to reset it at a different time.

How to Lessen Jet Lag

make less, decrease

1. Try not to become exhausted before you leave. Get plenty of sleep, and leave 85 enough time to get to the airport and check in without having to hurry.

2. Wear **loose** clothing, and take your shoes off while you are in your seat.

loose ≠ tight

3. Walk around the plane and move 90 around in your seat.

4. Figure out breakfast time in the time zone you are flying to. Four days before your flight, start a **feast** (eating a lot) and **fast** (eating nothing or very little) schedule. On the 95 fourth day before you fly, eat three heavy meals. If you drink coffee, tea, or cola drinks that contain **caffeine**, have them only between 3:00 and 5:00 p.m. On the third day before your flight, eat very lightly—salads, light soups, 100 fruits, and juices. Again, have drinks with caffeine only between 3:00 and 5:00 p.m. On the next to the last day before you leave, feast again. On the day before you leave, fast. If you are flying west, drink caffeinated drinks in the 105 morning; if you are going east, drink them between 6:00 and 11:00 p.m.

5. On the day you leave, have your first meal at the time people in the new time zone eat breakfast. If it is a long flight, sleep on the plane until the new breakfast time, and don't drink any alcohol. When you wake up, have a big meal. Stay awake and active, and eat at the new time zone hours.

A Vocabulary

signal	position	pressure	attack
alarm	experiments	event	jet lag
temperate	migrate	heartbeat	fast

1. Countries with ________________ climates have four different seasons.
2. A photovoltaic cell has to be in the right ________________ for the sunlight to enter.
3. A wedding is an important ________________ in anyone's life.
4. Students usually have to do ________________ in chemistry class.
5. Some people ________________ for religious reasons.
6. When the fire ________________ sounded, everyone left the building.
7. Doctors listen to a person's ________________ through a stethoscope to see if there are any irregularities.
8. High blood ________________ can cause a serious illness.
9. Pilots don't usually suffer from ________________ because they never stay in the new time zone very long.

B Vocabulary

rhythm	dawn	temperate	tides
feast	lessens	migrate	signal
pressure	caffeine	loose	experience

1. Chocolate, tea, coffee, and cola drinks contain ________________.
2. The police officer gave a ________________ for the cars to stop.
3. Some birds ________________ to a warmer climate in the winter.
4. The villagers prepared a ________________ to entertain the visiting government officials.
5. There are high and low ________________ in the ocean twice a day.
6. The sun rises at ________________.
7. ________________ is the opposite of *tight*.
8. Aspirin ________________ the effects of a headache.

C Vocabulary Review

stroke	stood for	tools	senses
units	projects	rolls	waves
guess	valuable	mild	surface

1. U.S.S.R. ________________ the Union of Soviet Socialist Republics.
2. A carpenter cannot work without ________________.
3. Water, light, and sound travel in ________________.
4. You can often use the context to ________________ what a word means.
5. Dust on the ________________ of a photovoltaic cell makes it work inefficiently.
6. Hearing is one of the five ________________.
7. A ball or other round object ________________.
8. This textbook has five ________________.
9. Biospheres are special ________________ at many environmental research laboratories.
10. Diamonds are ________________.

D True/False/Not Enough Information

_______ 1. *Jet lag* means your body is in one time zone but your biological clock is in another.
_______ 2. Plants begin producing nutrients when the sun rises.
_______ 3. Plants in Iceland and Greenland can produce nutrients twenty-four hours a day during the summer.
_______ 4. A biological clock gives birds the signal that it is time to migrate.
_______ 5. Animals that live near the sea search for food at night when it is safer.
_______ 6. The honeybees in the experiment reset their biological clocks.
_______ 7. After a few days, the bees probably changed their biological clocks to New York time.
_______ 8. The human biological clock affects many parts of the body.
_______ 9. Humans cannot change their biological clocks once they are set, but bees can.
_______ 10. You can decrease the effects of jet lag.

E Comprehension Questions

1. What makes desert plants produce seeds?
2. Why do birds wake at dawn?
3. How do honeybees know when a flower opens?
4. Why do they want to know when a flower opens?
5. What is the time difference between New York and Paris?
6. Why should you wear loose clothing on a long flight?
7. Why should you have breakfast at breakfast time in the new time zone on the day you leave?

F Main Idea

Copy or write a sentence for the main idea of these paragraphs.

1. Paragraph 4 (lines 17–26).
2. Paragraph 8 (lines 44–53).
3. Paragraph 10 (lines 58–63).
4. Paragraph 12 (lines 72–81).

G Word Forms: Adjectives

Both the **-ing** form of the verb (the present participle) and the **-ed** form (the past participle) are used as adjectives. The **-ed** form often shows that the noun received the action, or it describes how a person feels. The **-ing** form often shows some action that the noun took, or it describes an object or possibly a person. However, there are many exceptions.

David was **bored** because the movie was **boring**.
Tom is **interested** in stamps. He thinks stamps are **interesting**.
Mary is an **interesting** person because she can talk about a lot of different things.

Put the right form of each participle in each sentence.

1. (exhaust) Climbing a mountain is _________________ work.
2. (exhaust) Al was _________________ after the soccer game.
3. (demand) Mr. Davis is a very _________________ teacher. He makes the students work hard and do their best.
4. (alternate) There are two kinds of electric current, direct and _________________.
5. (trap) The _________________ animal couldn't escape.
6. (damage) A _________________ car needs to be fixed.
7. (guess) Children like to play _________________ games.
8. (fascinate) Monopoly is a _________________ game for some people.
9. (complicate) American football is a _________________ game.
10. (terrify) Being in an airplane crash is a _________________ experience.

H Word Forms: Semi- and Hemi-

Hemi- is a prefix that means **half**. **Hemisphere** is the most common word with this prefix.
Semi- is a prefix that means **half** or **partly**. These are some common words with this prefix:

semiconductor
semicolon (;)
semitransparent
semisolid (Toothpaste and ice cream are semisolid.)
semifinal (in sports competitions)

semifinalist
semitropical (Hawaii is semitropical, but it is not in the tropics.)
semiweekly (twice a week; some meetings are held semiweekly and some magazines are published semiweekly)
semimonthly (twice a month)
semiyearly (twice a year)
semiprivate (a hospital room with two or three patients)
semisweet (Some chocolate is semisweet.)

Use 6 of these words in interesting sentences.

I Prepositions

1. If you have ever flown ____________ several time zones, you have experienced jet lag.
2. You arrived ____________ a new time zone, but your body was still living ____________ the old zone.
3. You were wide awake and ready ____________ dinner ____________ the middle ____________ the night.
4. Plants and animals are all ____________ rhythm ____________ the natural divisions ____________ time.
5. ____________ the temperate zones ____________ the earth, trees lose their leaves ____________ fall as the days grow shorter.
6. Plants ____________ the desert may appear dead ____________ months or even years.
7. Some animals depend ____________ the sea for their food.
8. Some insects wake ____________ ____________ night.
9. Honeybees can tell ____________ the position ____________ the sun exactly when their favorite flowers open.
10. They put ____________ sugar water every morning ____________ 10:00 and noon.

J Connecting Words

Connect a sentence from the first column with one from the second column using **since, when, until**, or **even though**.

1. The bees were ready to eat.
2. It has been snowing.
3. Chris stopped drinking coffee in the evening.
4. Birds start singing.
5. A photovoltaic cell is efficient.

a. It was only 3:00 p.m. in New York.
b. It kept her awake.
c. It becomes dusty.
d. The sun went down.
e. The sun rises.

K Sequence

Put these sentences about the French experiment in the right order.

_______ a. The scientists took the bees to New York.
_______ b. Some French scientists did an experiment.
_______ c. They put the sugar water out at 8:00 p.m.
_______ d. They put the sugar water out at 10:00 a.m. and noon.
_______ e. The bees looked for food at 3:00 p.m. New York time.
_______ f. The bees took a week to find the food at a different time.
_______ g. The bees came every evening at 8:00 p.m.

L Guided Writing

Write one of these two short compositions.

1. What does "biological clock" mean? Give examples.
2. Describe a time when you experienced jet lag.

Unit 5

Medicine and Health

Early to bed and early to rise makes a man healthy, wealthy, and wise.
—Benjamin Franklin

A clinic

Headaches

Pre-reading Questions

1. How often do you have headaches?
2. What causes you to have a headache?
3. How do you treat your headaches?

Context Clues

1. After Isamu got hit in the nose with a baseball, his nose started to **swell**.
   a. get bigger b. smell c. alarm
2. Old Mr. Rossi's **vision** is getting bad, so he wears strong glasses.
   a. health b. ability to see c. blood pressure
3. Doctors do not know how to **cure** some diseases.
   a. make better b. do research on c. protect
4. Maria's hair hangs down into her eyes. She keeps pushing it back off her **forehead**.
   a. the top part of the face
   b. the top of the head
   c. the part of the face under the eyes
5. There are five **patients** waiting to see the doctor.
   a. people who are very calm
   b. people who have a medical problem
   c. people who are studying medicine

1

Headaches

Some little man is inside your head, **pounding** your brain with a **hammer**. Beside him, a rock musician is playing a drum. Your head feels as if it is going to explode. You have a **headache**, and you think it will never go away.

Doctors say there are several kinds of headaches. Each kind begins in a different place and needs a different treatment.

hammer

One kind starts in the **arteries** in the head. The arteries **swell** (get larger) and send **pain** signals to the brain. Some of these headaches start with a change in **vision** (ability to see, sight). The person sees wavy lines, black dots, or bright spots in front of the eyes. This is a warning that a headache is coming. The headache occurs on only one side of the head. The vision is **blurred**, and the person may **vomit** from the pain. These headaches, which are called **migraine** headaches, are more frequent in women than in men. Sleep is the best **cure** for them.

Cluster headaches, which also start in the arteries, are called cluster headaches because they come in clusters or groups for 2 or 3 months. Then there are no more for several months or even years. A cluster headache lasts up to 2 hours and then goes away. At the beginning of the headache, the eyes are red and watery. There is a **steady** (continuing) pain in the head. When the pain finally goes away, the head is **sore**. Men have more cluster headaches than women do.

painful

The **muscle** headache, which starts in the muscles in the neck or **forehead**, is caused by **tension**. A person works too hard, is **nervous** about something, or has problems at work, at school, or at home. The neck and head muscles become tense, and the headache starts. A muscle headache usually starts in the morning and gets worse as the hours pass. There is a steady **pain**, pressure, and a bursting feeling. Usually **aspirin** doesn't help a muscle headache very much.

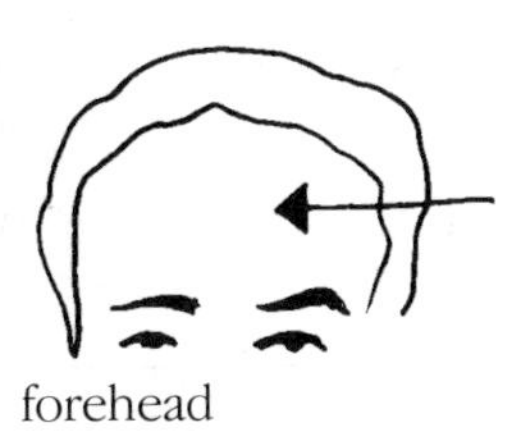

forehead

About 90 percent of all headaches start in the head and neck muscles. Another 10 percent start in the arteries.

How do doctors treat headaches? If a person has frequent headaches, the doctor first has to decide what kind they are. Medicine can help, but there are other ways to treat them.

The doctor asks the patient to analyze his or her daily living patterns. A change in diet or an increase in exercise might stop the headaches. If the patient realizes that difficulties at home, at work, or at school are causing the tension, it might be possible to make changes and decrease these problems. Psychological problems and even medicine for another **physical** problem can cause headaches. The doctor has to discuss and analyze all these patterns of the **patient's** life. A headache can also be a signal of a more serious problem.

of the body

Everyone has headaches from time to time. In the United States alone, up to 50 million persons each year go to the doctor because of headaches. If you have a headache, and it continues over several days, or keeps **recurring**, it is time to talk to a doctor. There is no magic cure for headaches, but doctors can control most of them because of recent research.

occurring again

A Vocabulary

pounded	swells	blur	migraine
clusters	sore	forehead	aspirin
recur	drums	pain	hammer
artery	nervous	vomit	cures

1. ________________ means to *happen again*.
2. If your arm is ________________, it hurts. You have a ________________ in your arm.
3. The ________________ is the top part of the face.
4. ________________ helps some kinds of headaches.
5. When we went to our friend's apartment, we knocked and then ________________ on the door, but no one answered.
6. One kind of headache is called a ________________.
7. A ________________ is one kind of tool.
8. When you put air in a bicycle tire, the tire ________________ until it fits the wheel exactly.
9. After the TOEFL test, the students gathered in small ________________ to talk about it.
10. Do you feel ________________ when you have to take a test?

B Vocabulary

ache	warned	blurred	arteries
vomit	cures	physical	swell
steady	patients	muscles	tense
vision	hammer	drum	forehead

1. When you are sick and in pain, your stomach may protest and make you ________________.
2. The teacher ________________ the children that they had to behave or there would be no party.
3. People in the hospital are called ________________.
4. While Pat was swimming, she got water in her eye. Everything looked ________________.
5. Students feel ________________ before an important exam.
6. Tension in the ________________ of the neck can cause a headache.
7. The farmers were happy when a ________________ rain continued all night.

8. __________ carry blood from the heart to the rest of the body.
9. Today there are __________ for many diseases that used to kill people.
10. People with poor __________ wear glasses or contact lenses.
11. You may get a *stomach* __________ if you eat too much.
12. A complete __________ examination is necessary for anyone entering the army.

C Vocabulary Review: Antonyms

Match the opposites.

1. fiction __________	a. point
2. scatter __________	b. import
3. active __________	c. nonfiction
4. fact __________	d. unclear
5. obvious __________	e. microscope
6. last __________	f. run out
7. export __________	g. gather
8. loose __________	h. increase
9. fast __________	i. inactive
10. lessen __________	j. theory
	k. feast
	l. tight

D Multiple Choice

1. When someone sees black dots or wavy lines, this is a change in ______.

   a. blurring b. clusters c. vision

2. A migraine headache causes ______.

   a. blurred vision
   b. red and watery eyes
   c. a bursting feeling

3. ______ is the best cure for migraines.
   a. Sleep b. Aspirin c. Arteries
4. ______ have more headaches that leave the head sore.
   a. Women b. Men c. Older people
5. A ______ headache starts in the morning and gets worse.
   a. migraine b. cluster c. muscle
6. Tension causes a ______ headache.
   a. migraine b. cluster c. muscle
7. The ______ headache is the most common.
   a. migraine b. cluster c. muscle
8. Medicine is ______ headaches.
   a. the best treatment for
   b. not usually helpful for
   c. one way to treat
9. A change in a patient's life patterns can ______.
   a. help cure headaches b. cause headaches c. both a and b

E Comprehension Questions

1. Describe a migraine headache.
2. Describe a cluster headache.
3. Describe a muscle headache.
4. Which kind of headache affects more women than men?
5. What are some things that can cause a muscle headache?
6. If you have a headache, will aspirin help?
7. Why does a doctor analyze the life patterns of a headache patient?
8. How many people each year in the United States go to a doctor for headaches?

F Main Idea

Write the main idea of these paragraphs.

1. Paragraph 2 (lines 6–8).
2. Paragraph 3 (lines 9–20).
3. Paragraph 8 (lines 48–59).

G Word Forms

	Verb	Noun	Adjective	Adverb
1.	press	pressure		
2.	experiment	experiment	experimental	experimentally
3.	migrate	migration		
4.	lessen	least	less	
5.	warn	warning		
6.	pain	pain	painful painless	painfully painlessly
7.	swell	swelling	swollen	
8.	recur	recurrence		
9.	tense	tension	tense	tensely
10.	prove	proof	proven	

1. Mr. Johnson has high blood __________________. He has to take medicine every day.
2. Physics teachers do __________________ in class.
3. Scientists study the __________________ of birds.
4. The pain of some headaches is __________________ by aspirin.

5a. A fire alarm is a __________________ to leave the building.

5b. A __________________ light tells people there is danger.

6. A broken arm is __________________.
7. Dan hurt his hand and now it is __________________.
8. After the fifth __________________ of a bad headache, Mark went to a doctor.
9. __________________ causes muscle headaches.
10. Scientists have __________________ that photovoltaic cells convert sunlight directly into energy. This was __________________ some years ago.

H Scanning

Scan the text to put these sentences in the right column. Write both the letter of the sentence below and the number of the line in the text where you find the idea.

	Migraine	Cluster	Muscle
a. They come in groups.			
b. It starts in the neck or forehead.			
c. It is caused by tension.			
d. There is a change in vision.			
e. There may not be any for several years.			
f. Aspirin doesn't help.			
g. Sleep helps.			
h. It occurs on only one side of the head.			
i. It lasts for 2 hours or less.			
j. Problems at work can cause it.			

I Noun Substitutes

What do these words stand for?

1. page 234 line 2 him ________________
2. line 4 it ________________
3. line 14 this ________________
4. line 20 them ________________
5. line 21 which ________________
6. page 235 line 31 which ________________
7. line 48 his or her ________________
8. line 66 them ________________

J Articles

1. Beside him, ______ rock musician is playing ______ drum.
2. Each kind begins in ______ different place and needs ______ different treatment.
3. One kind starts in ______ arteries in ______ head.

4. ______ arteries swell and send ______ pain signals to ______ head.
5. Some of these headaches start with a change in ______ vision.
6. ______ person sees ______ wavy lines, ______ black dots, or ______ bright spots in front of ______ eyes.
7. This is a warning that ______ headache is coming.
8. ______ headache occurs on only one side of ______ head.
9. ______ vision is blurred and ______ person may vomit from ______ pain.
10. ______ sleep is ______ best cure for them.

K Verb + Adjective

These verbs are usually followed by an adjective: **be, feel, become, seem, act, appear, look, smell, taste**.

She is sick.
She feels sick.
She became sick a week ago.
He seems tired.
He acts tired.
He appears tired.
He looks tired.
It smells good.
It tastes good.

Use each verb in an interesting sentence.

L Guided Writing

Write one of these two short compositions.

1. Describe the different kinds of headaches.
2. Discuss ways to treat and cure headaches.

Sleep and Dreams

LESSON

Pre-reading Questions

1. **What is the girl dreaming about?**
2. **Think about your dreams. How often do you dream? Do you dream in color or in black and white? What language do you dream in?**
3. **Do you think dreams come true?**

Context Clues

1. Saudi Arabia has **a great deal of** petroleum.
   a. some b. a lot of c. too much

2. **At times** you can feel a rock musician pounding a drum in your head.
   a. sometimes b. at a certain hour c. always

3. Tom always **confuses** Nissan cars with Hondas.
   a. signals b. mixes up c. introduces

4. Billy is 5 years old. Sometimes he wakes up in the middle of the night and cries. He has **nightmares**.
   a. bad dreams b. drums c. alarm clocks

5. Love, hate, and anger are **intense** feelings.
   a. strong b. opposite c. mild

6. Children from ages thirteen to nineteen are **adolescents**.
   a. young b. teenagers c. grownups

7. Mary has a bad **habit** of playing with her hair all the time.
   a. something that bothers her
   b. morning activity
   c. something she does often

2

Sleep and Dreams

"Oh sleep! it is a gentle thing,
Beloved from pole to pole."

Samuel Taylor Coleridge, a famous British poet, wrote these words over 100 years ago. Most people would agree with him. Sleep is very important to humans; the average person spends 220,000 hours of a lifetime sleeping. Until about thirty years ago, no one knew much about sleep. Then doctors and scientists began doing research in sleep laboratories. They have learned **a great deal** by studying people as they sleep, but there is still much that they don't understand.

a lot

Scientists study the body characteristics that change during sleep, such as body temperature, brain waves, blood pressure, **breathing**, and heartbeat. They also study rapid eye movement (REM). These scientists have learned that there is a kind of sleep with REM and another kind with no rapid eye movement (NREM).

taking air in and out of the body

NREM is divided into three **stages**. In stage one, when you start to go to sleep, you have a pleasant floating feeling. A sudden noise can wake you up. In stage two, you sleep more deeply, and a noise will probably not wake you. In stage three, which you reach in less than thirty minutes, the brain waves are less active and stretched out. Then, within another half hour, you reach REM sleep. This stage might last an hour and a

half and is the time when you dream. For the rest
30 of the night, REM and NREM alternate.

Body movement during sleep occurs just before the REM stage. The average person moves about thirty times during sleep each night.

Sleep is a biological need, but your brain
35 never really sleeps. It is never actually blank. The things that were on your mind during the day are still there at night. They appear as dreams, which people have been discussing for centuries. **At times** people believed that dreams had magical
40 powers or that they could tell the future.

sometimes

Sometimes dreams are terrifying, but they are usually a collection of scattered, **confused** thoughts. If you dream about something that is worrying you, you may wake up exhausted,
45 **sweating**, and with a rapid heartbeat. Dreams have **positive** effects on our lives. During a dream, the brain may **concentrate** on a problem and look for different solutions. Also, people who dream during a good night's sleep are more likely
50 to remember newly learned skills. In other words, you learn better if you dream.

mixed up

with water on the skin

opposite of *negative*

Researchers say that **normal** people may have four or five REM **periods** of dreaming a night. The first one may begin only a half hour
55 after falling asleep. Each period of dreaming is a little longer, the last one lasting up to an hour. Dreams also become more **intense** as the night continues. **Nightmares** usually occur toward dawn.

lengths of time

bad dreams

60 People dream in color, but many don't remember the colors. Certain people can control some of their dreams. They make sure they have a happy ending. Some people get relief from bad dreams by writing them down and then changing
65 the negative stories or thoughts into positive ones on the written paper. Then they study the paper before they go to sleep again.

Many people talk in their sleep, but it is usually just confused half sentences. They might feel **embarrassed** when someone tells them they were talking in their sleep, but they probably didn't tell any secrets.

Sleepwalking is most common among children. They usually grow out of it it by the time they become **adolescents**. Children don't remember that they were walking in their sleep, and they don't usually wake up if the parent leads them back to bed.

teenagers

Some people have the **habit** of **grinding** their teeth while they sleep. They wake up with a sore jaw or a headache, and they can also damage their teeth. Researchers don't know why people talk, walk, or grind their teeth while they are asleep.

There are lots of jokes about snoring, but it isn't really funny. People **snore** because they have trouble breathing while they are asleep. Some snorers have a condition called sleep **apnea**. They stop breathing up to thirty or forty times an hour because the throat muscles relax too much and block the airway. Then they breathe in some air and start snoring. This is a dangerous condition because, if the brain is without oxygen for 4 minutes, there will be **permanent** brain damage. Sleep apnea can also cause irregular heartbeats, a general lack of energy, and high blood presure.

always, forever

Most people need from 7½ to 8½ hours of sleep a night, but this varies with individuals. Babies sleep eighteen hours, and old people need less sleep than younger people. If someone continually sleeps longer than normal for no **apparent** reason, there may be something physically or psychologically wrong.

obvious, adjective for *appear*

You cannot save hours of sleep the way you save money in the bank. If you have only 5 hours of sleep for three nights, you don't need to sleep

an extra 9 hours on the weekend. And it doesn't do any good to sleep extra hours ahead of time when you know you will have to stay up late.

What should you do if you have trouble sleeping? Lots of people take sleeping pills, but these are dangerous because they are habit-forming. If you take them for several weeks, it is hard to stop taking them.

Doctors say the best thing is to try to relax and to avoid bad habits. If you always go to bed and get up at about the same time, this sets a good and healthy rhythm in your life. Caffeine keeps people awake, so don't drink caffeine drinks in the evening. Smoking and alcohol can also keep you awake. You may have trouble sleeping if you have a heavy meal just before you go to bed. Eat earlier in the evening.

You may also have trouble sleeping if you have a problem or something else on your mind. This is when you need to relax. As you lie in bed, tense the muscles in your feet and then relax them. Continue up the body, tensing and relaxing the muscles until you reach the head. Start with the feet again if you are still tense. Then remember some pleasant experience you had and relive it. If you are thinking about a problem or about something exciting that is going to happen the next day, get up and write about it. That will help take it off your mind. You can also get up and read or watch television. Be sure to choose a book or show that is not too exciting, or you may get so interested that you won't want to go to sleep even when you feel sleepy.

Sleep is important to humans. We spend a third of our lives sleeping, so we need to understand everything we can about sleep.

Sleep well! Sweet dreams!

A Vocabulary

stage	periods	normal	habit
oxygen	embarrassed	confused	positive
a great deal	at times	sweat	concentrate
nightmare	grinds	snore	block

1. It is hard to ________________ on your homework if your roommate is playing loud music.
2. It is not ________________ to have a headache for a week. You should go to a doctor.
3. In the first ________________ of a volcanic eruption, the volcano sends out smoke.
4. A ________________ is a bad dream.
5. ________________, a headache begins without warning.
6. The school day is divided into several ________________, one for each class.
7. Marcel ________________ coffee with a coffee grinder.
8. Sylvia has a ________________ of having a cup of coffee as soon as she gets home from work.
9. Hard exercise makes you ________________.
10. A Mercedes-Benz car costs ________________ of money.
11. Do you ________________ when you sleep?
12. There is no reason to feel ________________ when you make a mistake in class.

B Vocabulary

confused	positive	intense	adolescents
jaws	apnea	apparently	sweat
habit	block	permanently	breathe

1. Fish can ________________ underwater; people cannot.
2. The ________________ summer heat of the Arabian Desert can be very dangerous if you're not careful.
3. *Negative* is the opposite of ________________.
4. David was ________________ about the date, so he missed the meeting.
5. Someone with sleep ________________ stops breathing many times during the night.

6. An immigrant plans to stay in a new country ________________.
7. The professor seems to be very busy. ________________, he has a lot of work to do.
8. ________________ are not children, but they are not grown up either.
9. The teeth are in the upper and lower ________________.
10. A car accident can ________________ a highway.

C Vocabulary Review

Match the words with the definitions.

1. melt ________________	a. middle
2. mid- ________________	b. distance across a circle
3. strip ________________	c. fingerprint
4. crops ________________	d. reasonable
5. diameter________________	e. no moving parts
6. inexhaustible________________	f. change from a solid to a liquid
7. solid-state________________	g. can be seen through
8. source________________	h. because
9. transparent________________	i. long, thin piece
10. boundary ________________	j. place
11. since ________________	k. happening
12. position ________________	l. can't be used up
13. event ________________	m. place something comes from
	n. border
	o. any plants a farmer grows

D True/False/Not Enough Information

_______ 1. We spend about a third of our lives sleeping.

_______ 2. Researchers now understand nearly everything about sleep.

_______ 3. NREM sleep comes before the REM stage.

_______ 4. After the three stages of NREM, REM lasts the rest of the night.

_______ 5. Dreams occur during the REM stage, but the brain is normally blank the rest of the time.

_______ 6. A dream about an unhappy event can change your heartbeat.
_______ 7. Nightmares occur early when dreams are short.
_______ 8. People dream in color.
_______ 9. Sleep apnea is the cause of some snoring.
_______ 10. It is a good idea to sleep a few extra hours on the weekend if you know you have a lot of work to do the next week.
_______ 11. Five or 6 hours of sleep is enough for some people.
_______ 12. The best thing to do when you have trouble sleeping is to take sleeping pills.

E Comprehension Questions

1. How have researchers learned about sleep?
2. What does REM mean?
3. At what stage of sleep do people move around?
4. How do dreams change as the sleep period continues?
5. Why do people feel embarrassed if they talk in their sleep?
6. Can sleepwalking be dangerous? Give a reason for your answer.
7. Why do some people grind their teeth while they sleep?
8. How can sleep apnea cause brain damage?
9. Name three things that can keep you awake.
10. How does a problem keep you from sleeping?

F Main Idea

Find or write a sentence for the main idea of these paragraphs.

1. Paragraph 3 (lines 20–30).
2. Paragraph 5 (lines 34–40).
3. Paragraph 7 (lines 52–59).
4. Paragraph 13 (lines 97–103).

G Scanning

Write short answers and the line numbers for these questions.

1. In what stage of NREM can a sudden noise wake you up?
2. Why do people snore?
3. Why is it a bad idea to take sleeping pills?

4. How many REM periods of dreaming do normal people have?
5. What did some people use to believe about dreams?
6. What should you do if you can't sleep because you are thinking about an exciting event the next day?
7. Is it possible to control dreams?
8. Can you save up on sleep ahead of time?
9. How many times a night does an average person move?
10. How many hours a day do babies sleep?

H Connecting Words

Connect a sentence from the first column with one in the second using these words: **before, after, although,** and **since**.

1. People move in their sleep.	a. You go to bed.
2. Scientists don't know everything about sleep.	b. It isn't really funny.
3. We shouldn't laugh about snoring.	c. The REM stage begins.
4. Don't eat a heavy meal.	d. This sets a rhythm in your life.
5. Go to bed and get up at about the same time.	e. They have learned a lot in the last thirty years.
6. The REM stage begins.	f. The NREM stage begins.

I Missing Words

Write any word that is correct for the blanks.

1. Sleep is very important ______ humans; ______ average person spends 220,000 hours of ______ lifetime sleeping.
2. Then doctors ______ scientists began doing research ______ sleep laboratories.
3. They have learned ______ great deal ______ studying people as they slept.
4. Scientists study ______ body characteristics that change ______ sleep.
5. NREM ______ divided ______ three stages.
6. You reach stage three ______ less ______ thirty minutes.
7. Sleep is ______ biological need, ______ your brain never really sleeps.

8. _____ things that were _____ your mind during _____ day are still there _____ night.
9. _____ times people believed _____ dreams had magical powers _____ that they could tell _____ future.
10. _____ is possible _____ dreams have _____ positive effect _____ our lives.

J Word Forms

	Verb	Noun	Adjective	Adverb
1.		(ab)normality normalcy	(ab)normal	(ab)normally
2.		habit	habitual	habitually
3.	concentrate	concentration		
4.	confuse	confusion	confused	
5.		intensity	intense	intensely
6.		adolescence	adolescent	
7.	breathe	breath breathing	breathless	breathlessly
8.		permanence	permanent	permanently
9.	loosen	looseness	loose	loosely
10.	(dis)appear	(dis)appearance	apparent	apparently

1a. ________________, classes begin at 8:00, but there is a special meeting today.
1b. Sleep apnea is an ________________.
2. The present tense is used for ________________ actions.
3a. Great ________________ is necessary for the game of chess.
3b. Most of Australia's population is ________________ on the east coast.
4. There was a lot of ________________ about the new class schedule, but now it is all cleared up and things are going smoothly. At first, the students were ________________.
5. Susan feels everything very ________________.
6. ________________ is a difficult time for young Americans and their parents.
7. Tom spoke ________________ because he was so excited.
8. Nora married a German and is going to live ________________ in Germany.
9. Carol ________________ her belt because it was too tight.

10. The plane got in an hour ago, but Mohammed hasn't called. ________________ he wasn't on it.

K Guided Writing

Write one of these two short compositions. Paraphrase the information as much as possible.

1. When and why do we dream?
2. If a person has trouble sleeping, what can he or she do about it?

Health Care and Epidemics

LESSON

Pre-reading Questions

1. **When you are sick, do you take medicine? Why? How can people prevent disease?**
2. **Have you ever been in a place that was having an epidemic? What did the people do about it?**

Context Clues

1. When you are sick, you feel **miserable**.
   a. very bad b. very reasonable c. very steady

2. Today there are **remedies** for diseases that people used to die from.
   a. medicines b. cures c. aspirin

3. The teacher was busy, so Katsuko **volunteered** to help the new student with her schedule.
   a. did it without being asked
   b. waited for the teacher to choose someone
   c. avoided

4. What is the **worth** of learning Japanese if you are never going to Japan?
   a. occurrence b. value c. pain

5. Mr. Thomas sat reading the paper. **Meanwhile**, his 2 children were doing their homework.
   a. unpleasant b. although c. at the same time

3

Health Care and Epidemics

Everyone suffers from disease at some time or another. However, millions of people around the world do not have good health care. Sometimes they have no money to pay for medical treatment. Sometimes they have money, but there is no doctor. Sometimes the doctor does not know how to treat the disease, and sometimes there is no treatment. Some people are afraid of doctors. When these conditions are present in large population centers, **epidemics** can start.

Epidemics can change history. Explorations and wars cause different groups of people to come into **contact** with each other. They carry strange diseases to each other. For example, when the Europeans first came to North and South America, they brought diseases with them that killed about 95 percent of the Native American population.

touch

People are very afraid of unknown things, especially diseases. People have all kinds of ideas about how to prevent and treat diseases. Some people think that if you eat lots of onions or garlic, you won't get sick. Others say you should take huge amounts of vitamins. Scientific experiments have not proved most of these theories.

However, people still spend millions of dollars on vitamins and other probably useless treatments or preventatives. Some people want **antibiotics**
30 whenever they get sick. Some antibiotics are very expensive. Much of this money is wasted because some diseases are caused by a **virus**. Viruses are even smaller than bacteria, and they cause different kinds of diseases. Antibiotics are useless
35 against viruses.

Because of their fear, people can be **cruel** to victims of disease. Sometimes they fire them from their jobs, throw them out of their apartments, and refuse them transportation services.
40 In the **plague** epidemics a few hundred years ago, people simply covered the doors and windows of the victims' houses and left them to die inside, all in an effort to protect themselves from getting sick.

a very serious disease carried by insects

45 Doctors know how most epidemic diseases spread. Some, like **tuberculosis**, are spread when people **sneeze** and **cough**. The explosive cough or sneeze sends the bacteria shooting out into the air. Then they enter the mouth or nose
50 of anyone nearby.

Others are spread through human contact, such as on the hands. When you are sick and blow your nose, you get viruses or bacteria on your hands. Then you touch another person's
55 hand, and when that person touches his or her mouth, nose, or eyes, the disease enters the body. Some diseases spread when people touch the same dishes, towels, and furniture. You can even pick up a disease when you touch things in public
60 buildings.

Other diseases are spread through insects, such as flies, **mosquitoes**, and **ticks**.

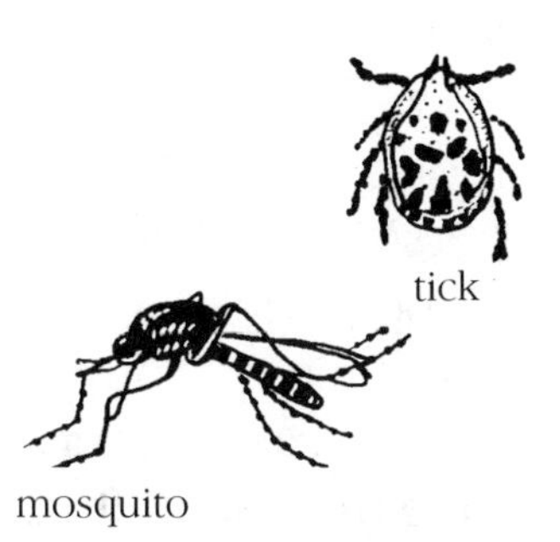

One disease that causes frequent, worldwide epidemics is **influenza**, or flu for short. The
65 symptoms of influenza include headache and

sometimes a runny nose. Some victims get sick to their stomachs. These symptoms are similar to symptoms of other, milder diseases. Influenza can be a much more serious disease, especially
70 for **pregnant** women, people over sixty-five, and people already suffering from another disease, such as heart problems. About half of all flu patients have a high body temperature, called a **fever**. Flu is very **contagious**. One person
75 catches the flu from another person; it doesn't begin inside the body as heart disease does.

pregnant

goes easily from a sick person to a healthy person

Sometimes medicine can **relieve** the symptoms. That is, it can make a person cough less, make headaches less intense, and stop noses
80 from running for a while. However, medicine can't always cure the disease. So far, there is no cure for many diseases and no medicine to prevent them. People have to try to prevent them in other ways.

make better

85 Some diseases can be prevented by **vaccination**. A liquid vaccine is **injected** into the arm or taken by mouth and the person is safe from catching that disease. Other diseases can be prevented by good health habits, such as drinking
90 only clean water, boiling water that might carry disease, and washing the hands often.

injected

Epidemics usually start in areas of large population. Poor people in big cities who live crowded together in **miserable** conditions have
95 the most health problems. They often have the least education about disease prevention. If they know what to do, they often do not have the money to do it. For example, it is difficult for a person who has no electricity to refrigerate food
100 or boil drinking water. With no money, the person can't even buy soap to wash his or her hands.

very bad, inferior

Disease prevention costs much less than disease treatment. It seems completely illogical, but some countries like the United States spend much

105 more health-care money on treatment for diseases than on programs to prevent disease in the first place. Most doctors and other hospital workers stay in their **institutions**. Only a few doctors go out into the streets of the poor areas to 110 educate the people. Only a few doctors and some nurses vaccinate people and supervise them to make sure they take their medicine. Most people who help the poor people with their health problems are **volunteers**.

115 How can you use all this information for your own good health? When someone you know becomes ill, try to avoid physical contact with that person. If you get sick yourself, keep your towel and dishes separate from everyone else's. Try not 120 to touch things that belong to others. Don't touch other people, and don't shake hands. Explain why, however; you don't want people to think you are impolite. Wash your hands often if you are ill or if anyone around you is ill.

125 Researchers continue searching for a way to cure or prevent epidemic diseases. **Meanwhile**, it is **worth** the money for governments to provide preventive health care for all of their people. Preventing epidemics is much cheaper than stop- 130 ping them after they have started and thousands of people are ill.

A Vocabulary

cough	epidemics	cruel	institutions
meanwhile	contagious	sneeze	miserable
plague	antibiotics	vaccinations	influenza

1. ________________ is also called the flu.
2. Some diseases are spread when people ________________ and ________________
3. When you have a headache, you probably feel ________________.
4. Babies should receive ________________ to prevent common childhood diseases. Then they won't catch these ________________ diseases.
5. Governments should provide health care. ________________, they should give money for new research into the causes of disease.
6. ________________ kill thousands, even millions, of people worldwide.
7. Hospitals and universities are examples of ________________.
8. It is very ________________ to put a sick person out of his or her house into the street to live.
9. The ________________ epidemics killed half the population of Europe before ________________ were discovered.

B Vocabulary

fever	contact	tuberculosis	symptoms
relieve	volunteer	viruses	injected
pregnant	worth	mosquitoes	ticks

1. When your temperature is above normal, you have a ________________.
2. There is no physical ________________ in tennis. The players don't touch each other while they play.
3. Ms. Davis is ________________. She is going to have a baby in May.
4. How much is gold ________________ today?
5. Diseases caused by ________________ cannot be cured with antibiotics.
6. Some vaccines are ________________ into the arm; others are taken by mouth.

7. Aspirin can ________________ some headaches.
8. What are the ________________ of a cold? How do you know you have one?
9. Thousands of people ________________ to work for the Red Cross without pay.
10. Diseases carried by ________________ and ________________ enter the victim's blood through the bites of these insects.
11. ________________ enters the body when the victim breathes the air coughed out by a sick person.

C Vocabulary Review

raw materials	attacked	dawn	tide
hammer	drummer	record	pounded
swell	arteries	forehead	recurring

1. Blood is carried from the heart through the ________________.
2. If you hit your thumb with a ________________, the thumb will probably ________________ up.
3. Sometimes the sky is beautiful at ________________.
4. Tom got hit in the ________________ with the ball.
5. The army ________________ at dawn to surprise the enemy.
6. Rita has a ________________ pain in the stomach. It comes and goes.
7. The waves move higher up on the beach as the ________________ comes in.
8. Iron and cotton are ________________.
9. Dan ________________ on the table to get everyone's attention.
10. Every rock music band has a ________________.
11. The government keeps a ________________ of the birth of every child.

D Multiple Choice

1. Coughing is a ______ of tuberculosis.
   a. miserable b. epidemic c. symptom

2. Medicine ______ a disease.
   a. can cure
   b. can relieve the symptoms of
   c. can prevent

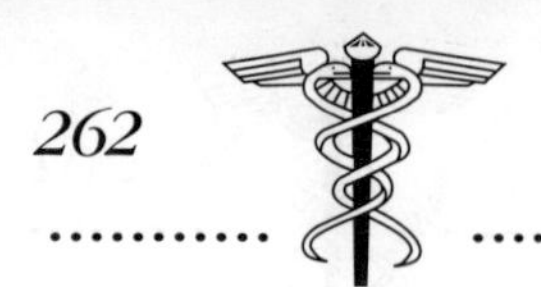

3. Without the Europeans, North and South America ______
   a. would probably have more Native Americans
   b. would probably have no diseases
   c. would probably have no wars

4. Which one of these sentences is not true?
   a. Antibiotics can be expensive.
   b. Antibiotics have saved the lives of many sick people.
   c. Antibiotics will help cure viruses.

5. ______ prevent some diseases.
   a. There is no vaccine to
   b. You can have a vaccine injected into your arm to
   c. Both a and b

6. Tuberculosis spreads ______.
   a. by hand contact
   b. when people cough and sneeze
   c. when people don't eat garlic

7. The best way to avoid epidemics is to ______.
   a. lock sick people up inside their houses
   b. take lots of vitamins
   c. provide health care for people crowded in cities

E Comprehension Questions

1. Name the symptoms of influenza.
2. What does medicine do for diseases?
3. Is it worth the expense to take extra vitamins?
4. How do epidemics spread?
5. How can epidemics change history?
6. Do you think you should or should not shake hands with someone who is ill? Why?
7. Why do poor people have the most health problems?
8. Why do people who live in the city have more health problems than people who live in the country (outside of cities)?
9. How can humans prevent diseases from becoming epidemics?

F Main Idea

What is the main idea of these paragraphs?

1. Paragraph 2 (lines 12–19).
2. Paragraph 4 (lines 36–44).
3. Paragraph 6 (lines 51–60).
4. Paragraph 10 (lines 85–91).

G Cause and Effect

Write the effect for each of these causes.

Cause	Effect
1. A virus enters the body.	
2. People take medicine.	
3. A person with tuberculosis coughs.	
4. A vaccine is injected into the body.	
5. A student drinks from a sick roommate's glass.	

H Word Forms

	Verb	Noun	Adjective	Adverb
1.		(im)politeness	(im)polite	(im)politely
2.		cruelty	cruel	cruelly
3.	relieve	relief		
4.	volunteer	volunteer	(in)voluntary	(in)voluntarily
5.	inject	injection		
6.		pregnancy	pregnant	
7.		contagion	contagious	contagiously
8.	lengthen	length	long	
9.	reason	reason	(un)reasonable	(un)reasonably

1. The idea of ________________ is different from one country to another.

2a The government was known for its ________________ to prisoners.

2b. It is ________________ to hit a very old or sick person.

3. Mary felt ________________ when she found out her daughter had arrived safely at her grandparents' home.

4. Mark did not go into the army ________________. He went because it is the law that all young men must serve in the army.

5. Children don't like to have ________________.
6. A human ________________ lasts 9 months.
7. Heart trouble is not ________________.
8. In the spring, the days start to ________________.
9. Mehdi was very angry. We tried to ________________ with him, but he was completely ________________ and wouldn't listen at all.

I Two-Word Verbs

Learn these two-word verbs and then fill in the blanks with the right words. Use the correct verb form.

grow out of —A child stops doing or feeling something as she or he grows older.
get out of —avoid doing
show up —appear, arrive
put off —delay
read up on —get facts and information on a subject by reading

1. Hiroko always tries to ________________ talking in front of the class because she doesn't like to do it.
2. Tom had planned to go to the shopping center today, but he ________________ it ________________ until the weekend because he's so busy.
3. Children ________________ sleepwalking when they become adolescents.
4. Marge is going to ________________ photovoltaic cells because she wants to know more about them.
5. Bob didn't ________________ for the party until almost midnight.

J Articles

Write an article in each blank if one is needed.

1. However, millions of _____ people around _____ world do not have _____ good health care.
2. Sometimes _____ doctor does not know how to treat _____ disease, and sometimes there is no _____ treatment.

3. ______ people have all kinds of ______ ideas about how to prevent and treat ______ diseases.
4. ______ explosive cough or sneeze sends ______ bacteria shooting out into ______ air.
5. Then they enter ______ mouth or nose of ______ anyone nearby.
6. Some diseases spread when ______ people touch ______ same ______ dishes, ______ towels, and ______ furniture.
7. Some countries like ______ United States spend much more health-care money on ______ treatment for diseases than on programs to prevent ______ disease in ______ first place.

K Summarizing

Summarize paragraph 3, lines 20–35. Use your own words to tell the main idea in no more than 3 or 4 sentences.

L Guided Writing

Write one of these two short compositions.

1. You are a health-care worker who is going into a poor area of a big city. You have seen several cases of tuberculosis and influenza this month. You are going to try to prevent an epidemic among the people in this area. What will you say to the people?

2. A government official in your country has asked you for your suggestions about improving health care. What will you say to the official?

CPR

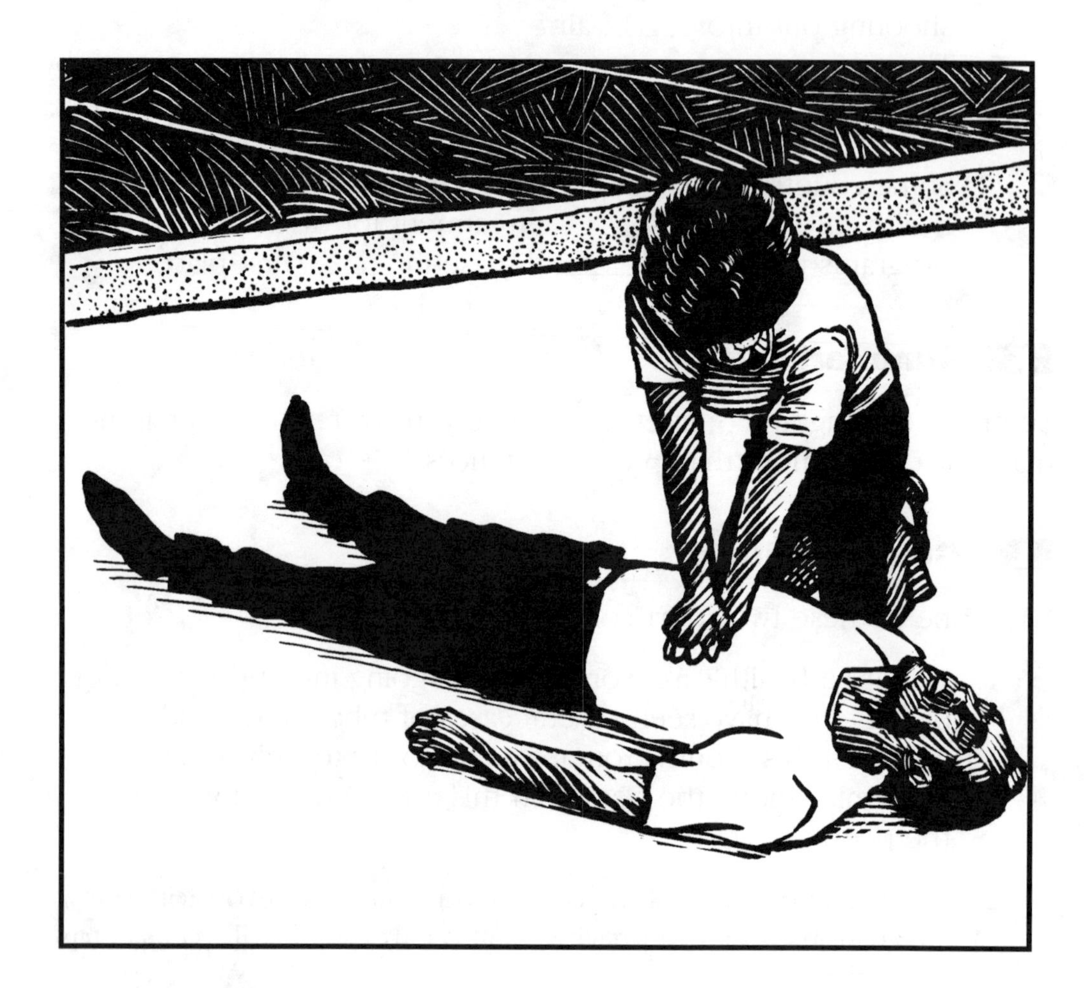

LESSON

Pre-reading Questions

1. What is happening in the picture?
2. Do you think the woman is a doctor, or could she be a person without medical training?
3. Do you know how to do CPR? If not, would you like to learn?

Context Clues

1. Adults should never **strike** children, even when the children misbehave.

   a. hit b. help c. block

2. Alice couldn't swim very well, but she swam way out into the middle of a lake. She was too tired to swim back to shore, and her head kept going under the water. Finally, she **drowned**.

   a. rested b. died in the water c. concentrated

3. How do you think your parents will **react** when you tell them you are going to marry someone from another country?

   a. act in response to a situation
   b. start doing some activity
   c. act again

4. Paul has a new car and **so do I**.

   a. I am too. b. I do too. c. I think it is true.

5. A photovoltaic cell cannot **function** efficiently if it has dust on it.

   a. breathe b. confuse c. work

6. Take this umbrella with you **in case** you need it.

   a. if maybe b. such as c. at times

4

CPR

CPR stands for cardiopulmonary **resuscitation**. *Cardio* is a medical word for *heart. Pulmonary* is a medical word for **lungs**. *Resuscitate* means to *bring back to life*. CPR starts someone's lungs and heart **functioning** again after they have stopped.

working

It is an amazing idea that there is a cure for sudden death. It is equally amazing that this magic is not done by today's high technology. Any ordinary person can do it. You use your own lungs to breathe into the patient's mouth and start his or her lungs working. You push on the heart with your hands to make it start beating again. It is as easy as that.

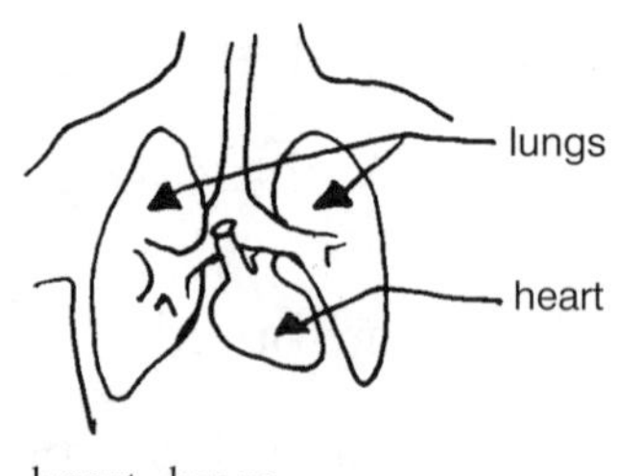

heart, lungs

The heart is a large muscle that **pumps** blood through the arteries. It is **located** in the center of the **chest** behind the **breastbone**. The lungs are at either side of the heart. Air enters the nose and mouth and moves through the airway to the lungs, bringing oxygen into the body. As the blood moves through the lungs, it picks up the oxygen and carries it to the cells throughout the body. At the same time that the blood picks up the oxygen, it leaves carbon dioxide as a waste material, and the lungs breathe it out through the airway.

found

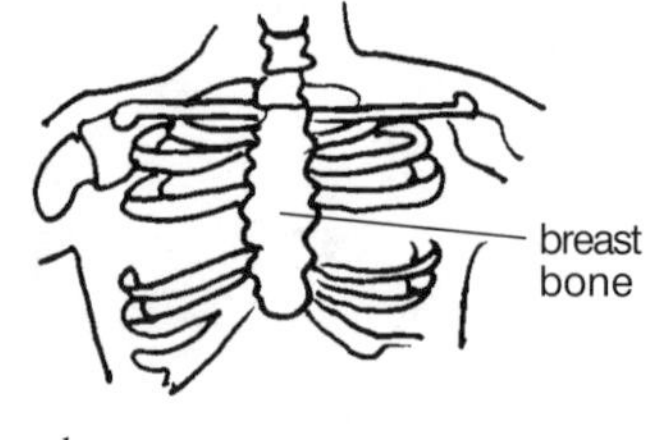

chest

When the heart stops beating, or a person stops breathing, this whole **process** stops. No

oxygen is taken into the body, and the blood
30 doesn't move through the arteries. CPR can start
the process moving again.

There are several situations when CPR is needed. It can be used when a person has a heart attack and the heart stops. A heart attack occurs
35 when the heart cannot get enough oxygen. This usually happens because one of the two arteries to the heart has become narrow or completely blocked. The heart muscle cells that are supplied with oxygen by that artery die because they stop
40 receiving oxygen.

One of the symptoms of a heart attack is a feeling of pressure and tightness or aching in the center of the chest. It lasts longer than 2 minutes, and it may come and go. The person having a
45 heart attack may also start sweating, feel weak, be short of breath, and feel like vomiting. However, there may be no symptoms at all; the heart may stop suddenly, and the person may stop breathing. If CPR is started immediately, it may bring the
50 person back to life.

CPR can also be used when a person receives an electric **shock**. If enough electricity enters the body, the person dies immediately. CPR can resuscitate the person. An electric shock usually
55 happens to someone who has been working carelessly with electricity. It can also happen if lightning **strikes** a person. — hits

A third situation is **drowning**, or dying in water, which happens most often in the summer
60 when many people go swimming. Children can also drown when they are left alone near a swimming pool. A person trained in CPR can help a person start to breathe after clearing the water out of the airway.

65 These are the three most common causes of sudden death when CPR can be used. There are others less common. Someone in a burning

building may breathe in too much smoke and not get any oxygen into the lungs. Some people have
70 an intense **reaction** to certain drugs or to the **sting** of a bee or some other insect, and the heart and lungs stop functioning.

CPR is an example of **first aid**. An ordinary person can take a first aid class and learn what to
75 do until the patient receives professional help. This might mean helping someone until an **ambulance** comes. Then professionals can use their equipment to **take charge** of the patient. Or it might mean giving first aid and then taking the
80 patient to a doctor. CPR can keep a person alive until he or she reaches a hospital.

help

ambulance

When you give CPR, you breathe directly into the patient's mouth. Then you press on the heart in the center of the chest. You continue alternat-
85 ing these two actions.

CPR is easy to learn, but you shouldn't learn it from a book. You should receive instruction in a class where you can practice in front of the instructor until you do it correctly. As you know,
90 if the brain is without oxygen for 4 minutes, there will be permanent brain damage. It is necessary to start CPR immediately when a person stops breathing, or as soon as possible. You have to know how to do it quickly and well.

95 If someone in your family has heart trouble, if you go swimming a lot, or if you plan to work with electricity, you should learn CPR. In fact, everyone should learn it, **in case** they ever need it.

Where can you learn it? The Red Cross has
100 CPR classes, many hospitals teach it, and so do some university student health centers. If there are no classes where you live, ask the Red Cross or a nearby hospital to organize a class.

CPR is worth learning. It can give you the
105 chance to save someone's life.

A Vocabulary

resuscitation	located	pump	strike
sting	first aid	react	lung
breastbone	process	drown	function

1. The heart is directly behind the ________________.
2. Village people often have to ________________ water by hand.
3. Volcanoes are ________________ in clusters.
4. Hail and snow are formed by a similar ________________.
5. A bee ________________ is painful.
6. The ________________ of the heart is to pump blood through the arteries.
7. Children should wear a life preserver when they are around water so they can't ________________.
8. Anyone can learn to give ________________. You don't have to be a doctor or nurse.
9. The *R* in CPR stands for ________________.

B Vocabulary

chest	so	in case	shock
lungs	breastbone	process	ambulance
take charge	strike	reaction	drown

1. The ________________ are in the chest and ________________ is the heart.
2. In baseball, if a player tries to hit the ball and misses it, it is called a ________________ even though he didn't hit the ball.
3. An electric ________________ can kill a person.
4. An ________________ is used to take patients to a hospital.
5. A strong ________________ to a drug can kill a person.
6. Edward volunteered to ________________ of arranging food for the party.
7. The natural ________________ that makes garbage disappear is slowed at landfills because the garbage gets no air or water.
8. You cannot save up sleep ahead of time ________________ you need it later.

C Vocabulary Review: Synonyms

Match the words that mean the same.

1. worth ________	a. a lot
2. miserable ________	b. blur
3. contagious ________	c. teenager
4. a great deal ________	d. catching
5. at times ________	e. vision
6. nightmare ________	f. forever
7. confused ________	g. value
8. adolescent ________	h. location
9. permanently ________	i. painful
10. sore ________	j. unhappy
11. dawn ________	k. sometimes
12. position ________	l. sunrise
	m. mixed up
	n. bad dream

D True/False/No Information

_____ 1. *Resuscitation* is a medical word.
_____ 2. Sudden death can be cured only by using today's technology.
_____ 3. The arteries take carbon dioxide out of the lungs.
_____ 4. Carbon dioxide enters the lungs through the airways.
_____ 5. CPR can be used in cases of drowning.
_____ 6. CPR can help a person with sleep apnea.
_____ 7. A common situation when CPR is needed is with a reaction to an insect sting.
_____ 8. First aid is an example of CPR.
_____ 9. Everyone should get a book about CPR and learn how to do it.
_____ 10. You should call an ambulance before you start CPR.

E Comprehension Questions

1. What is the function of the lungs?
2. What are the symptoms of a heart attack?
3. What are the three most common situations when CPR is needed?

4. What is first aid?
5. How can CPR prevent brain damage?
6. What professionals work with patients?

F Main Idea

What is the main idea of these paragraphs?

1. Paragraph 2 (lines 7–14).
2. Paragraph 11 (lines 82–85).
3. Paragraph 13 (lines 95–98).

G Prepositions and Two-Word Verbs

1. Some children are afraid of the dark, but they grow ______ ______ it.
2. CPR stands ______ cardiopulmonary resuscitation.
3. CPR is a method ______ starting someone's lungs and heart again ______ they have stopped.
4. It is an amazing idea that there is a cure ______ sudden death.
5. You should take a class ______ CPR. Don't put it ______.
6. No oxygen is taken ______ the body, and the blood doesn't move ______ the arteries.
7. One ______ the symptoms ______ a heart attack is a feeling ______ pressure and tightness or aching ______ the center ______ the chest.
8. CPR may bring the person back ______ life.
9. Then professionals can take charge ______ the patient.
10. Some people have an intense reaction ______ the sting ______ a bee.

H Compound Words and Two-Word Verbs

Make a compound word by joining a word from the first column with one from the second column. More than one answer is correct for several of the words. Some of these are also written separately as two-word verbs.

1. break	a. in	______________________
2. stand	b. down	______________________
3. work	c. work	______________________

4.	check	d. mate	______________
5.	sun	e. rise	______________
6.	home	f. night	______________
7.	sleep	g. by	______________
8.	out	h. grow	______________
9.	life	i. walk	______________
10.	over	j. way	______________
11.	air	k. time	______________
12.	room	l. out	______________

I Word Forms

	Verb	Noun	Adjective	Adverb
1.	resuscitate	resuscitation		
2.	locate	location		
3.	react	reaction		
4.	drown	drowning		
5.		similarity	(dis)similar	(dis)similarly
6.	relate	relation(ship)	relative	relatively
		relative	(un)related	
7.	medicate	medicine	medical	medically
8.	die	death	dead	
9.	light	lightning	light	
	lighten			
10.	tighten	tightness	tight	tightly

1. With CPR, you may be able to ______________ someone.
2a. The newspaper gave the time and ______________ of the university entrance exam.
2b. The Chemistry Building is ______________ next to the Physics Building.
3a. How would you ______________ if you saw someone drowning?
3b. There are machines to test your ______________ time when you are driving.
4. There were two cases of ______________ at the beach near our home last year.
5. What is the ______________ between snow and hail?
6a. What is the ______________ between changes in the family and population growth?

6b. Population growth in industrial countries is ________________ slow.

6c. Munir is ________________ to the Minister of Education.

7. Jane wants to go to ________________ college and become a doctor.

8. A heart attack doesn't always cause ________________.

9. Before it started to rain, there was a lot of thunder and ________________.

10. The little boy held ________________ to his father's hand.

J Summarizing

Write a summary of the text for this lesson. Write only the important information using 3 to 5 sentences.

K Guided Writing

Write one of these two short compositions.

1. What happens during CPR and how does it work?

2. What are some situations in which CPR is useful?

Cholesterol and Heart Disease

LESSON

Pre-reading Questions

1. Which of the three dinners is best for you? Why?
2. Which of the three dinners would you rather eat? Why?
3. Is it difficult or easy to change what you eat? Why?

Context Clues

Circle the letter of the best meaning of the **bold** word.

1. A student with short purple hair walked into the classroom. Everyone **stared** at him.
   a. talked b. swelled c. looked intensely
2. I like your new shirt. It's very **attractive**.
   a. pretty b. large c. permanent
3. That young man looks **familiar**. I think he attended my high school.
   a. like a member of a family
   b. like someone I know
   c. like a relative of mine
4. Paulo was **confident** that he could save someone's life after he took a CPR class.
   a. sure b. process c. volunteer
5. I ate a big dinner, but I feel a little hungry. Before I go to bed, I think I'll have a **snack**.
   a. big meal b. pizza c. small amount of food
6. Sharon said her new car was worth $30,000, but it only cost $20,000. She **exaggerated.**
   a. said it cost more than it did
   b. paid $30,000 for it
   c. didn't like her old car

5

Cholesterol and Heart Disease

Do you know your **cholesterol** level? Many people don't. A high level of cholesterol in the blood is an important **risk factor** for heart disease.

Some people say that the danger of heart disease is **exaggerated**. However, heart disease is a main cause of death in developed countries. Every year more than one million Americans have heart attacks, and half of them die. People with heart disease suffer chest pains that make simple activities, such as walking, shaving, or taking a shower, difficult.

exaggerated: said it is more than it is

Research has proven that cholesterol levels are connected with heart disease. One project in Massachusetts has studied the same group of men and women since 1948. The researchers have found that the people who have high levels of cholesterol have more heart attacks.

A natural substance in the blood, cholesterol comes from the liver. The amount of cholesterol is affected by diet and by physical qualities we **inherit** from our parents. One kind of cholesterol sticks fat to the walls of arteries, making them smaller and finally blocking them. It produces a condition called "hardening of the arteries," which causes heart attacks. With tiny cameras,

inherit: get

doctors can see blood circulating through the heart **valves**. **Angiograms** are x-rays of the heart arteries. They show fat deposits and blockages caused by high cholesterol.

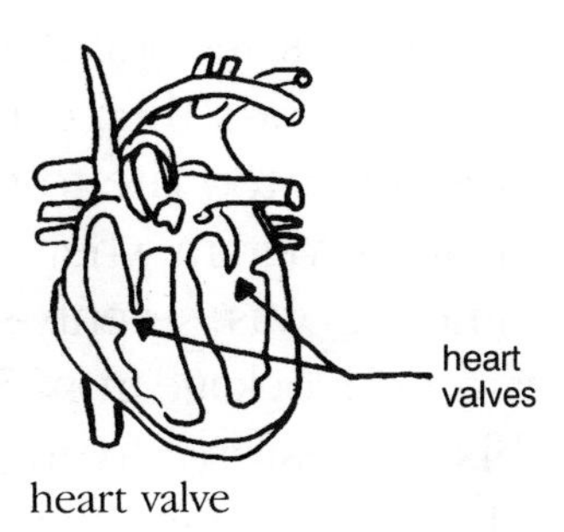

heart valve

30 Heart disease begins in children as young as 3 years old. It occurs earlier in boys than in girls. Nearly half of teenagers have some fat deposits on their artery walls. Heart disease develops faster if we have high cholesterol levels and also 35 smoke.

What is a safe level of cholesterol? Adults have a high risk of heart attack if their cholesterol level is above 240 milligrams per deciliter of blood. Below 200 is better. In the Massachusetts 40 study, no one with a cholesterol level below 150 has ever had a heart attack. However, about half of American adults have cholesterol levels above 200.

To lower our cholesterol level, we must change our eating habits. Anything that comes 45 from an animal is high in fat and high in cholesterol. The American Heart Association National Cholesterol Education Program says that fat should be no more than 30 percent of our diet. Blood cholesterol levels start to fall after 2 to 3 50 weeks of following a low-cholesterol, low-fat diet. Dietary changes alone can result in a 10 percent **reduction** of the average person's cholesterol level. **Aerobic** exercise helps, too. Artery blockage can be reduced by as much as 40 percent 55 through changes in diet and amount of exercise.

making smaller

for example, walking running, swimming

We must educate everyone, including children in elementary schools. We must teach them responsibility for their health through classes in nutrition and aerobic exercise. For example, the 60 smart **snack** is fruit. Children must be served fruit in the school cafeteria, along with low-fat meals. Schools must send **recipes** home with the children. Parents must include children in planning and preparing meals and shopping for food.

something small and fast to eat

instructions for cooking

65 Adults, including persons over the age of sixty-five, can lower their cholesterol by 30 or 40 percent. It is never too late to change. One man began his health program when he was seventy-three. By the time he was seventy-seven, he had lowered his 70 arterial blockage from 50 percent to 13 percent and his cholesterol from 320 to 145 without drugs. He went on a vegetarian diet with only 10 percent fat, plus programs to reduce **stress** and get more exercise.

75 A low-cholesterol diet that cuts out most animal products and high-fat vegetables may be **unfamiliar** to people. The Heart Association says to use no added fat of any kind. Don't fry food in oil. Cook it in water, vinegar, or vegetable 80 water. Learn about grains and vegetables. Avoid egg yolks (the yellow part of the egg). Eat potatoes, beans, low-fat vegetables, and fruit. People often **complain** about low-fat diets before they have had time to get used to them. Food can taste 85 good without cream, butter, and salt. You can use olive oil, mustard, fresh **herbs**, or yogurt instead.

strange, unknown

say you don't like something

A new diet can cause general **anxiety**, when people feel worried and nervous about what is going to happen. They must learn to **deal with** 90 the changes in their lives. Sometimes major changes in diet or lifestyle are easier than minor ones because the results are bigger and faster. Fast results **encourage** us.

cope with

give hope

How can you control the amount of fat in 95 your diet if you eat in restaurants? Restaurants must provide healthy meals that are low in fat, salt, and cholesterol. A diet is a **personal** thing. Restaurant owners should not make customers feel embarrassed because they want to follow a 100 diet that is good for them. Restaurant owners must learn to give equal **service** to customers on a healthy diet. Some restaurants have items on the menu marked with a heart to show that they

private, about oneself

are low in fat, cholesterol, salt, or sugar. A few
105 restaurants serve only these recipes.

Heart disease causes one out of every four deaths in East Harlem in New York City. The East Harlem Healthy Heart Program is an educational program. It has 2 goals: to get people to change
110 their diets and to find volunteers to help run educational activities. One way it educates is by street shows. Actors wear costumes and carry big pieces of plastic fat. They entertain so people will listen. Groups of children perform songs and
115 dances that educate people about heart disease and diet. Volunteers lead walking and exercise groups to show people how to begin exercising.

Volunteers also stand in supermarkets to **suggest** healthy food choices to shoppers. The
120 volunteers have shoppers taste two kinds of milk to see which tastes better. Most people are surprised that the low-fat milk tastes better than the whole milk. Shoppers are encouraged to buy low-fat milk instead of whole milk.

give ideas about

125 Education costs money, but it also brings results. In 1983, only 35 percent of the American public knew their cholesterol levels. By 1990, 65 percent of the people had had theirs checked.

People feel better if they lower their choles-
130 terol through diet. Healthy people are more **confident**. They are more **attractive** to themselves, as well as to others. Their friends **stare** at them because they look so healthy.

pretty, handsome

look intensely

We can prevent heart disease by living a
135 healthful lifestyle and eating the right kind of diet. If people don't do this, two out of three men and women in America will eventually get heart disease.

A Vocabulary

confidence	anxiety	stare	herbs
aerobic	risk	encouraged	valve
unfamiliar	inherited	personal	snack

1. John's parents ________________ him to stay in school even though his grades were not very good.
2. ________________ exercise is good for the heart.
3. Is it impolite to ask someone ________________ questions?
4. Students often suffer from ________________ before an exam.
5. ________________ improve the taste of food.
6. Some people are ________________ with a low-fat diet.
7. Mark ________________ red hair from his mother.
8. It is impolite to ________________ at people.
9. If you drive carelessly, you take a ________________.
10. I'm hungry now, but it's 2 hours until dinner. I think I'll have a ________________.
11. Open the ________________ so the water will flow freely through the pipes.
12. If you are sure of yourself, you have ________________ in yourself.

B Vocabulary

factor	suggestion	deal with	complains
attractive	reduction	service	angiogram
exaggerated	cholesterol	recipe	stress

1. Most television stars are ________________.
2. ________________ occurs naturally in the blood.
3. A ________________ in how much fat you eat might make you healthier.
4. Please give me a copy of that delicious ________________.
5. One of the students made a good ________________ for what we could do in the International Day program.
6. It is difficult to ________________ a child who doesn't behave well.
7. Smoking is a ________________ in many diseases of the heart and lungs.
8. Tom said he earned $1000 a week, but he is really paid only $800. He ________________.

9. The doctor wants my mother to have an ________________ to see if her arteries are blocked.
10. Ali always ________________ that he has too much homework.
11. This restaurant has good food, but the ________________ is slow.
12. The ________________ of running away from the dog was too much for the old man, and he had a heart attack.

C Vocabulary Review

Match the words with the definitions.

1. nervous ________________
2. period ________________
3. habit ________________
4. meanwhile ________________
5. fever ________________
6. pregnant ________________
7. location ________________
8. strike ________________
9. react ________________
10. drown ________________
11. solar ________________
12. observe ________________

a. length of time
b. at the same time
c. stage
d. act in response to something
e. grind
f. hit
g. watch
h. die in water
i. anxious
j. usual action
k. high body temperature
l. of the sun
m. place
n. going to become a mother

D True/False/Not Enough Information

______ 1. Around 500,000 Americans die each year from heart disease.

______ 2. More than twice as many people had their blood cholesterol levels checked in 1990 as in 1983.

______ 3. Smoking can be a risk factor for heart disease.

______ 4. No direct relationship has been proven between high cholesterol levels and heart attacks.

______ 5. Girls have no risk of heart disease.

______ 6. Low-fat diets always taste bad.

______ 7. Children should learn more responsibility for eating healthful food.

_______ 8. People usually feel good about going on a new diet.
_______ 9. It can be easier to change our diet a lot than to change it a little.
_______ 10. Old people shouldn't bother to change their eating habits because it's too late for it to do them any good.
_______ 11. Most people think that whole milk tastes better than low-fat milk.

E Comprehension Questions

1. What are some symptoms of heart disease?
2. What is "hardening of the arteries"? How is it connected with high cholesterol?
3. Why are angiograms useful?
4. At what age does heart disease start?
5. What level of cholesterol is believed to be safe?
6. How long does it take for cholesterol levels to start to drop?
7. How can schools help teach children healthy eating habits?
8. How can parents help teach children healthy eating habits?
9. What are some ways to reduce fat in your diet?
10. Describe the East Harlem Healthy Heart Program.

F Main Idea

What is the main idea of these paragraphs?

1. Paragraph 4 (lines 18–29).
2. Paragraph 6 (lines 36–42).
3. Paragraph 9 (lines 65–74).
4. Paragraph 12 (lines 94–105).

G Word Forms

	Verb	Noun	Adjective	Adverb
1.		anxiety	anxious	anxiously
2.	encourage	encouragement	encouraged	
3.	discourage	discouragement	discouraged	
4.		stress	stressful	stressfully
5.	personalize	person	personal	personally
6.		stupidity	stupid	stupidly
7.	attract	attraction	(un)attractive	(un)attractively

	Verb	Noun	Adjective	Adverb
8.	inherit	inheritance		
9.	familiarize	familiarity	(un)familiar	familiarly
10.	suggest	suggestion		
11.	complain	complaint		complainingly
12.	exaggerate	exaggeration		
13.	serve	service		

1. The students waited _________________ to hear the results of the test.

2a. A shy child needs a lot of _________________ to build self-confidence.

2b. Marie was _________________ by the results of her physical exam after a long illness.

3. Michael felt _________________ when he wasn't accepted at the university that was his first choice.

4. Joan felt a lot of _________________ when she stood before the class and began her speech.

5a. If you tell the salesperson your initials, the store will _________________ your new suitcase at no extra charge.

5b. _________________, I like my initials on my luggage.

6. Marie felt _________________ because she did the exercise without reading the directions and did it all wrong.

7. Honey _________________ flies and ants. Flies and ants _________________ by honey.

8. Tom _________________ a small business and some money from his father when his father died. His friend received a large _________________ from his favorite uncle.

9. If you _________________ yourself with the language center before the first day of classes, you will not get confused about where you should go.

10. I _________________ that we take a CPR class this month. That's a good _________________.

11. If you have any _________________ about the television set you bought, take it back to the store.

12. To say that you couldn't go to sleep at all last night is an _________________. You are _________________.

13. A waiter _________________ food in a restaurant.

H Irregular Verbs

Learn these verbs. Then put the right verb forms in the blanks, using the first verb in the first sentence, and so on.

Simple	Past	Past Participle
1. tear	tore	torn
2. light	lit or lighted	lit or lighted
3. lie	lay	lain
4. swell	swelled	swollen
5. grind	ground	ground
6. strike	struck	struck
7. sting	stung	stung
8. stick	stuck	stuck
9. deal	dealt	dealt

1. Alice ________________ her new blouse.
2. Dan ________________ a fire in the living room fireplace.
3. In some countries, it is the custom to ________________ down for a rest in the middle of the day.
4. Ms. Baxter's hand is ________________ because she shut it in the car door.
5. Mr. Thomas ________________ some fresh coffee beans and made coffee.
6. When the clock ________________ 12, the people in the street knew it was noon.
7. Bob got ________________ by a bee.
8. The roadrunner ________________ out its head in front when it runs.
9. Mr. Nevins is a car dealer. He ________________ in new and used cars.

I Two-Word Verbs: Review

1. Sixteen people showed ______ for volleyball practice.
2. Never put ______ until tomorrow what you can do today.
3. What time does your plane get ______?
4. Were you brought ______ in the city or country?
5. The teacher left ______ one student on the class list.
6. Do you dress ______ for dinner at an expensive restaurant?
7. Look ______! There's a hole in the sidewalk.

8. I have to read ______ ______ a subject for my speech.
9. Kim had ______ a warm jacket so I knew it was cold outside.
10. The Bakers have to buy new shoes for their daughter. She grew ______ ______ her old ones.
11. We tried to get ______ ______ helping out our cousin, but we had to do it.

J Context Clues

These words have more than one meaning. Circle the letter of the best meaning of the **bold** word. Choose the meanings of the words as they are used in these sentences.

1. Mr. Becker has worked in the **field** of computer science for 10 years.
   a. an area of specialization
   b. a place where animals or plants are raised
   c. the place where baseball is played
2. Carolyn is often late for class because she has to walk **so far** from her apartment.
   a. until now b. such a long distance c. far enough
3. There are 2.2 **pounds** in a kilo.
   a. the unit of English money
   b. hits or strikes
   c. a unit of weight
4. Trappers sometimes **cure** the skins of the animals they catch before they sell them.
   a. dry and prepare for use
   b. make better
   c. a kind of medicine
5. The **current** value of gold is $321.
   a. the movement of electricity
   b. at this time
   c. the movement of a stream of water in the ocean

6. I know that it isn't **so**.
   a. very
   b. too
   c. true

7. Ali and Muhammed live in a large apartment **complex** near the university.
   a. related group of buildings
   b. complicated
   c. anxiety

K Summarizing

Write a summary of the text for this lesson. Write only the important information using 3 to 5 sentences.

L Guided Writing

Write one of these two short compositions.

1. You are going to start an educational program about heart disease in your area. How will you do this?

2. Your doctor told you that you have to lower your cholesterol. Give a detailed plan of how you will follow the doctor's suggestion.

Vocabulary

Index of Explanations Grammar and Word Forms